Masques In Jacobean Tragedy

God shewes his judgements which were good, for every man to marke: When as you see the wicked man, lie trapt in his owne warke.

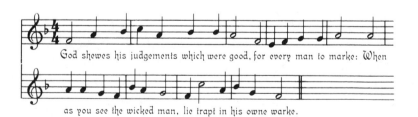

God shewes his judgements which were good, for every man to marke: When as you see the wicked man, lie trapt in his owne warke.

Psalm 9:16, versification for congregational singing, from Thomas Sternhold and John Hopkins, *The Whole Booke of Psalms* (London, 1562), modernization by S. F. Johnson, Columbia University.

MASQUES IN JACOBEAN TRAGEDY

SARAH P. SUTHERLAND

AMS Press, Inc.
New York

PR
658
.M3
S9
1983

Library of Congress Cataloging in Publication Data

Sutherland, Sarah P.
  Masques in Jacobean tragedy.

  (AMS studies in the Renaissance, ISSN 0195-8011;
no. 9)
    Bibliography: p.
    Includes index.
    1. English drama—17th century—History and
criticism.   2. English drama (Tragedy)—History and
criticism.   3. Masques.   I. Title.   II. Series.
PR658.M3S9   1983   822'.0512'09   81-69122
ISBN 0-404-62279-8   AACR2

MANUFACTURED IN THE UNITED STATES
OF AMERICA

Acknowledgements

S. F. Johnson's name appears on the acknowledgement pages of dozens of books on English Renaissance literature. I take pleasure in humbly adding this volume to the large and growing collection of books, many of them distinguished contributions to their fields, that were conceived in the classrooms of this rigorous scholar and coaxed forth under the tutelage of this demanding though gentle taskmaster. I thank Professor Johnson for much of what there may be of value in the pages that follow. The lapses are dark things that I acknowledge mine.

Others at Columbia University have contributed in significant ways. Mathew Winston and Bernard Beckerman gave this work thoughtful and helpful readings in its several early stages, and Elizabeth Story Donno encouraged the development of exacting and sensitive approaches to Renaissance literature that I hope are adequately reflected here. My discussions of Renaissance works with Roland Marandino, Glenn Spiegel, and many others helped me formulate ideas about the broader aspects of masques within plays. Ann Paschke Landi read valiantly through the earliest version of this study and made useful stylistic suggestions. William B. Long, my editor at AMS and himself a former student of S. F. Johnson's, guided me through revisions with skill and care.

I am grateful also to my colleagues at Lake Erie College for cheerfully tolerating the intrusion of this project when more pressing business loomed. To my father and to the memory of my mother I owe a debt that can be but poorly repaid here. Belated but special thanks go to Tom Hart for his constant sense of perspective and for remaining, throughout this and all my endeavors of many years, a man in his wholeness wholly attending.

Table of Contents

Introduction

Masques Within Plays

When the architect In-and-In Medlay, formerly Vitruvius
Hoop and known also as Inigo Jones, is invited to prepare a masque
in Ben Jonson's *A Tale of a Tub* (1633), there occurs this brief
exchange:

> Pan   A Masque, what's that?
> Scriben   A mumming, or a shew.
>   With vizards, and fine clothes.
> Clench   A disguise, neighbor,
>   Is the true word: . . .[1]

Although Jonson's satire in this scene is pointed and specific, the
definitions of a masque given by Scriben and Clench are more
comprehensive than context alone might suggest. Jonson is making
wry fun not only of his old rival Inigo Jones, but also of the quite
popular convention of inserting a masque into a play. This device,
the masque within a play, is defined with admirable precision by
Scriben and Clench: it is at once show and disguise, simultaneously
a source of wonder and, Clench may be implying, a hothouse for the
seeds of woe. The "vizards" and "fine clothes" of Scriben's answer
suggest the glories of the masque which, at their most splendid, could
summon an admiration like Ferdinand's in *The Tempest*: "This is a
most majestic vision, and / Harmonious charmingly" (4.1.118-19).
But Clench's word is true indeed; the masque is also a disguise. In
those vizards and fine clothes there is opportunity for the most secret
of intrigues, including such perfidious plots as Supervacuo's in *The*

Revenger's Tragedy: "A masque is treason's licence, that build upon; / 'Tis murder's best face when a vizard's on" (5.1.181-82). In both its capacities—as majestic vision and as treason's license, as nuptial entertainment and as revengeful revels, as show and as disguise—the masque within a play served the myriad purposes of the English Renaissance dramatists.

The review of critical interpretations of masques in plays in the section following this makes it clear that the device has by now been adequately catalogued and categorized. There is no need for one more survey of scores of masques in plays or yet another attempt to group plays or label masques according to more or less fixed divisions. Both are forms of criticism that approach the inserted masque by way of the play containing it. What might prove both interesting and useful, however, is criticism that approaches the play by way of the masque it contains. The critical literature yields few such discussions, and those that exist are analyses of single plays.[2] The present study is an attempt to extend the value of such work by considering not one but several plays, all of which contain—among many other elements—a masque.

Some questions immediately arise. What exactly constitutes a masque within a play? How does one select plays from the many that contain masques? Having selected them, in what order does one discuss them?

There have been almost as many definitions of inserted masques as there have been studies of the device. All agree that the masque in drama must have one or more of the features peculiar to the court masque; the disagreement comes in distinguishing the necessary features from those that are merely sufficient. Here is Inga-Stina Ewbank's definition: "a ritual in which masked dancers, with or without a presenter, arrive to perform a dance, sometimes to sing, and nearly always to 'take out' members of the stage audience."[3] Here it is apparently essential only that the masked dancers arrive; whether they in fact carry out their intentions to perform seems beside the point. What Ewbank is doing, of course, is trying to admit to her province those masques that never make it to performance, for Renaissance drama is replete with masques that are announced but never seen, or that are aborted midway through. It is indeed important to allow for such masques, but doing so virtually guarantees an exceedingly loose definition.

Ewbank's definition, like most the others, defines the inserted masque by reference to the critic's understanding of what constitutes masque. Yet it seems far more expedient, and a good deal safer, to define the inserted masque by reference to the *play's* understanding of what constitutes masque. An inserted masque is anything so labeled by a character in a play. It may lack some or all of the features normally associated with masque, it may be interrupted by the intrusion of a revenger, it may be planned or rehearsed but never performed at all. But if it is called masque by a character in a play, then the critic has a sufficient condition to treat it as such.[4]

The selection of illustrative plays has sometimes been a vexing task for readers who find rich and exemplary masques in obscure plays but tantalizingly brief revels in major works. But if one is setting out to explore a play by way of its inserted masque (rather than the other way around), it seems best to begin with the plays most likely to reward such exploration. During the period when masques first flourished both at court and in the drama, the incontestably major plays containing masques were the great Jacobean tragedies of Marston, Tourneur, Beaumont and Fletcher, Webster, and Middleton. There are, of course, many other plays containing masques during this period, and a number of those are both interesting and important works of art. But the six plays examined here fall into a clearly definable group bound by common genre, by proximity in time, and, as critic after critic has observed, by a dramatic effectiveness that places them among the finest plays performed in the English theater.[5]

I examine three matters of essential background before turning to the individual plays. One is Thomas Kyd's *The Spanish Tragedy*, which provides the dramatic precedent (though not necessarily the source) for much of the woe and a good deal of the wonder of later masques in plays. Another is the court masque—from Elizabethan disguising to the Jacobean spectacles of Jones and Jonson—which begets masques within plays. Finally, there is the matter of the theater itself, undergoing in the early seventeenth century some of the more significant changes in its history. Some readers may find themselves walking through familiar territory in parts of this section, and I ask their indulgence. Those less conversant with this material may find my review a useful introduction to the individual plays and their masques. But even those well acquainted with the background might benefit from a reassessment of specific connections between the six plays I discuss and the theatrical factors most closely connected with the inserted masques in those plays.

The plays are discussed in the order of their dates of first performance.[6] This reflects a conviction that it is very difficult and not especially useful to impose categories according to, say, the masque's dramatic function (most have multiple functions not easily categorized). The use of chronological order should not, however, be interpreted as suggesting a line of development, decadence, or direct influence from one play to another. The last would be all but impossible to prove, and either of the first two would greatly oversimplify dramatic history.

Of the six major Jacobean tragedies examined here, one contains an inserted masque that is nearly as long and full as a Jacobean court masque, another has a masque that is little more than a hastily danced measure, while the other plays incorporate versions of the Elizabethan antic masque or the court revels. Each inserted masque is both a show and a disguise, but none is solely spectacle or merely a device. Each of the six masques is symbiotically connected to the central dramatic actions of the surrounding play, and each serves specific dramatic functions in order to achieve identifiable dramatic effects.

In Marston's *Antonio's Revenge* and in Tourneur's *The Revenger's Tragedy*, masquers avenge wrongs done them by those spectators the masques are meant to honor. Each masque serves the revenging hero as the opportunity to take a divinely ordained revenge while serving the playwright not just as a convenient device but as a logically, theologically, and dramaturgically sound way of resolving the revenge action in the play.

The long nuptial masque in Beaumont and Fletcher's *The Maid's Tragedy* serves as an ironic foil to the disastrous wedding night that follows. But the masque also anticipates disaster when it leaves unresolved the escape of Boreas, a development that threatens both its own internal logic and the union it is meant to celebrate.

The masque of madmen in *The Duchess of Malfi*, one of the tortures Duke Ferdinand sends to his imprisoned sister Duchess, is a variation of the revels of revenge. But instead of driving the Duchess mad, as Ferdinand had wished, the madmen leave her quite sane— Duchess of Malfi still. In the last act the Duke himself is mad: the unjust revenger Ferdinand is figuratively (as Marston's Piero and Tourneur's Supervacuo are literally) snared in his own masque.

During the masque in *Women Beware Women*, each revenger is caught in another's plot even as he catches a victim in his own. This complex and spectacular masque is carefully crafted so that the theater audience, while given advance knowledge of each individual plot, shares the conspirators' surprise at the way their plots fall together and hoist six people with their own petards.

The antic dance of madmen and fools in *The Changeling* is not only a rehearsal for Beatrice's nuptial revels but also the climactic scene of the subplot. Analysis of the way this dance was probably staged shows how it brings into one gripping action all of the subplot's characters. Moreover, the dance analogically reflects past actions in the main plot and (rather as the masque in *The Maid's Tragedy* anticipates later action in that play) serves as a fit prologue to the final discovery of the "changes" Beatrice has wrought.

The forms and functions of each of these six masques are determined far more by the masque's relationship to the encompassing play than by external pressures from Kyd's precedent, the court masque, theatrical conditions, or by any independently chartable history of the device. But whatever the terms of that individual relationship, the masque in tragedy is always both a show and a disguise, simultaneously wonder and woe, at once "tied to rules of flattery" and "treason's licence." It yokes violently together the decorum inherent in celebratory court entertainment with the indecorum of madness, mayhem, and murder. It is the product of—and it illuminates—a peculiarly Jacobean sensibility.

List of Editions

The following editions of the six plays under discussion are those from which quotations have been taken. Other editions consulted are listed in the bibliography. For plays other than these six and the works of Shakespeare, editions used are cited in the notes. All quotations from Shakespeare's plays come from *William Shakespeare: The Complete Works*, gen. ed. Alfred Harbage (Baltimore: Penguin, 1969).

In references to stage directions, I use the method introduced in The Revels Plays and followed in The Regents Renaissance Drama Series. Lines of a stage direction appearing at the beginning of a scene are numbered 0.1, 0.2, and so forth (e.g., 4.3.0.2). Those occurring elsewhere are given the number of the last line before the stage direction, followed by .1, .2, etc. (e.g., 4.3.87.2).

Beaumont, Francis, and John Fletcher. *The Maid's Tragedy*. Ed. Robert K. Turner, Jr. In *The Dramatic Works in the Beaumont and Fletcher Canon*. Gen. ed. Fredson Bowers. Vol. 2. Cambridge: Cambridge Univ. Press, 1970.

Marston, John. *Antonio's Revenge*. Ed. W. Reavley Gair. The Revels Plays. Baltimore: Johns Hopkins Univ. Press, 1978.

Middleton, Thomas. *Women Beware Women*. Ed. J. R. Mulryne. Revels. London: Methuen, 1975.

Middleton, Thomas, and William Rowley. *The Changeling*. Ed. N. W. Bawcutt. Revels. London: Methuen, 1958.

Tourneur, Cyril. *The Revenger's Tragedy*. Ed. R. A. Foakes. Revels. London: Methuen, 1966.

Webster, John. *The Duchess of Malfi*. Ed. John Russell Brown. Revels. London: Methuen, 1964.

A Note on Orthography

Most of the editions from which I have taken quotations use modern spelling, though a few, such as Turner's edition of *The Maid's Tragedy*, retain old spelling. I have left each text exactly as the editor has rendered it, sacrificing orthographical consistency to the belief that I should not rush in where an editor has chosen not to tread. Occasionally, as when quoting from the Geneva Bible or from Chambers' quotations of early material, I have expanded contractions and aligned j/i and u/v with modern usage. In quoting passages of secondary material, I have made British spellings conform to standard American practice; titles of articles, journals, and books are not altered.

One word sometimes presents special problems. Old spelling "mask" or "maske" may denote either the modern "mask" or modern "masque," and conversely the old spelling "masque" may be either "mask" or "masque." The context will usually give sufficient indication of which modern spelling to use, but occasionally, as in *The Duchess of Malfi*, modernizing editors will differ. In those cases, it is less important to choose one spelling over another than to remember that for the ear there is no difference. Both meanings are often denoted in the theater in a way that cannot work on the printed page.

1

The Critical Heritage

Although most of the more than one hundred inserted dramas in the Renaissance are masques (or truncated versions of masques), critical attention to the device has lagged behind interest in the dumb show and the play within a play. The dumb show was amply treated a decade ago by Dieter Mehl,[1] but no comparably thorough study has been published on inserted plays or masques. Short analyses of plays within plays abound, most concentrating inevitably on *The Spanish Tragedy* and *Hamlet*. Studies of masques in plays are seen far less often and tend, when they do appear, to be elaborate catalogues of plays containing masques. In recent years, however, perhaps because of a fashionable interest in forms of literary self-consciousness, the inserted masque has come under closer scrutiny, particularly in unpublished dissertations. The history of the criticism is one of narrowing focus: from early lists and descriptive catalogues that range through many plays to short but intense analyses of a single masque in a particular play.

Unannotated lists of plays containing masques are given in Paul Reyher's *Les Masques anglais*[2] and in Robert Stanley Forsythe's *The Relations of Shirley's Plays to the Elizabethan Drama*.[3] The lists are not identical—and neither is exhaustive—but together they provide the best available primary bibliography. Both lists give act and scene for the location of the inserted entertainment, but neither one distinguishes carefully among masque, play, and dumb show.

Surveys of inserted masques begin with the brief but suggestive contribution of E. K. Chambers.[4] Development of the device is here traced from *intermedii* of early Tudor drama through Shakespeare's contributions in *Love's Labor's Lost* and *Romeo and Juliet* to the appearance of masques in boy company plays of the early seventeenth century. Chambers devotes some attention to Jonson's *Cynthia's Revels*, stressing the fact that the very full masque in that play "is Elizabethan and antedates by some four years the first of the long series of Jonson's Jacobean masks" while in Jacobean drama "you get the mask as it was practiced at Elizabeth's court, rather than at that of James."[5] But Chambers allows these rather provocative observations to rest, concluding somewhat inexplicably that "as a rule the element of mask remains an episode, and does not dominate the play which admits it."[6] Here Chambers forgets *Women Beware Women* and plays such as *The Maid's Tragedy* where the domination of the masque has very little to do with plot and a great deal to do with tone, theme, and the dramaturgical manipulation of audience response.

But if Chambers seemed to discourage further exploration of the inserted masque, Enid Welsford's important study of the masque at court[7] very nearly ended it altogether. In the few pages given to the drama, Welsford concentrates almost wholly on a vague "masque influence . . . permeating the form and spirit of tragedy in a way that is easier to feel than to define."[8] What exactly it is that Welsford feels is never quite explained. The imprecision enables her to dispense summarily with the inserted masque: ". . . even when the masque did not actually bring about the catastrophe, it deepened the horror, and brought with it a stifling atmosphere of intrigue and corruption. All this is too well known to need any further emphasis."[9]

Others have fortunately felt that the functions of masques in plays could indeed use further emphasis. F. S. Boas, for example, treats a few masques in his article on plays within plays.[10] But he stops with *The Tempest*, asserting that the play within a play disappears with Prospero's pageant.[11] It does not disappear, of course: Massinger's *The Roman Actor* and Middleton's *Women Beware Women* come a good decade after Shakespeare's last play.

Nearly thirty years elapsed before David Laird set out to correct the assumptions of Chambers, Welsford, and Boas. Laird's unpublished dissertation[12] is the first full-length study of the masque in English Renaissance drama. The study ranges over the whole of Renaissance theater: after preliminary chapters on the development of the masque and the functions of inserted drama from Medwall's *Fulgens and Lucrece* to Greene's *James IV*, Laird considers masque in the popular drama of the 1590s, in Jacobean tragedy, and in Jacobean comedy. While Laird treats too many plays with too little selectivity, he does make several important suggestions. A particularly intriguing hypothesis is that, in Jacobean tragedy, "the relation of the inserted masque to play may be that of masque to antimasque or conversely that of antimasque to masque."[13] The formula is a bit too neat, but it does nicely distinguish masques like those in *The Maid's Tragedy* or *Byron's Tragedy*, which are far more orderly than the action surrounding them, from masques like those in *The Duchess of Malfi* and *The Changeling*, where the masquers are madmen or fools. Laird's conclusion is also intriguing, if only because it illustrates a pervasive tendency to trot forth the reality-illusion dichotomy when talking about masques in plays. "The most characteristic effect of the inserted entertainment," Laird writes, "is to underwrite or authorize one level of dramatic representation through the use of another, to make stage action more plausible."[14] This kind of remark is encountered with enough frequency in the critical literature to warrant a separate examination later.

Another perspective on the inserted masque is suggested by Arthur Brown in an article written apparently without reference to Laird's dissertation.[15] In Brown's view, the masque proliferates in Jacobean tragedy as the quality of the drama declines. *Antonio's Revenge* and *The Revenger's Tragedy* succeed primarily in "cramming as much horror and complication as possible into the denouement," while in *Women Beware Women* "a love of tortuous plots and an obsession with wholesale slaughter for its own sake now predominate; the play or masque within a play is here no more than a convenience, failing to arouse any sense of its inevitability or of its theatrical effectiveness."[16] The masque has begun to signal decadence.

Dieter Mehl's interest in dumb shows in Elizabethan and Jacobean drama led him naturally to other forms of interior performance. His article "Zur Entwicklung des 'Play Within a Play' im elisabethanischen Drama"[17] is a useful study of the influence of *The Spanish Tragedy*'s "Soliman and Perseda" on later interior plays and masques. In another article,[18] however, Mehl sets aside the notion of *Entwicklung* (development or evolution) and organizes his material not by the date of a play but according to the type and function of its inserted drama. "Rather than outline once more the history of the play within a play," Mehl decided to "point out some distinctly different types of plays within plays that were developed by Elizabethan and Jacobean dramatists to suit their particular dramatic purposes."[19] Mehl classifies his inserted dramas according to their degrees of complexity. The simplest kind introduces a company of actors into a play (as in *Sir Thomas More*). More complicated forms are those in which characters from the "main" play perform in plays or masques at the climax of the drama. This last kind can be used to effect either reconciliation or revenge and therefore is found in both comedy and tragedy; Mehl cites Marston's *The Malcontent* and Middleton's *Your Five Gallants* as well as *Antonio's Revenge* and *The Revenger's Tragedy*. The article also looks at such "framed" plays as *The Rare Triumphs of Love and Fortune*, *The Taming of the Shrew*, and *James IV*. For the most part, Mehl successfully and pointedly avoids the problems of chronology and the restrictions of a rigid classification. In the end, though, he yields again to the idea that the play within a play went through a development from simplicity to complexity.[20] He concludes only that the device is

> a particularly striking example of the diffuse and experimental character of English Renaissance drama, of its astounding capacity for assimilating diverse conventions and for creating coherent and unified works of art out of seemingly contradictory elements of style.[21]

The first published study to deal solely with inserted masques appeared, appropriately, at the end of *A Book of Masques*.[22] Inga-Stina Ewbank's lengthy ramble through the annals of plays containing masques is still the most important and influential of the surveys. Her description of her subject, for example, is generally cited as the most comprehensive, if not the most precise: "plays in which an entertainment with the essential features of the court masque is definitely put on by one or more of the dramatis personae before other dramatis personae."[23] A footnote adds that "it is above all the taking-out, with its intermingling of stage audience and performers, that distinguishes the masque-within-a-play from the play-within-a-play and gives the former quite different dramatic possibilities from the latter."[24] Ewbank organizes her inserted masques in a fashion that may owe something to Mehl's rejection of the historical survey—"from the point of view of their contributions to the dramatic structure of the plays in which they are contained."[25] These contributions are of three sorts: allegorical, comic, and tragic. Under the first heading fall those masques that contribute to theme or tone or atmosphere but do not advance the plot; Ewbank places *The Maid's Tragedy*, *Timon of Athens*, and *The Tempest* in this group. Comic functions of the masque include furthering a love intrigue (*Love's Labor's Lost*), illustrating a moral or reforming manners (*Cynthia's Revels*), and effecting dramatic resolutions (*Satiromastix*, *The Lover's Melancholy*). Masques in tragedy tend to be used mainly for ironic reversals—sudden deaths in which "revenge has become ritual."[26] The predictable examples here are *Antonio's Revenge*, *The Revenger's Tragedy*, and *Women Beware Women*. Ewbank's categories are useful ones, but—like Laird before her—she does not select or discriminate enough for readers who already have mere catalogues available. Reviewing the book in which Ewbank's article appeared, Stephen Orgel complained that in her study "we are given the sort of essay which, when written by a graduate student, can be praised for its thoroughness and nothing else. It *does* mention *everything*."[27] Orgel's irritation is justifiable, but for those who can work their way through Ewbank's inclusiveness there are important concluding points. Most significantly, Ewbank is the first to state boldly that "no simple chronological development in the use of the inserted masque can be traced. . . ."[28] She also disagrees with critics like Brown who link the early seventeenth century's fascination with masques in plays to the drama's decline: "excepting Shakespeare's comedies, perhaps the finest, at once most complex and most integrated, use of the masque is in the comedies and tragedies of the first two decades of the seventeenth century."[29] Finally, she adds perspective to Laird's distinction between decorous masque and indecorous play when she concludes that "the masque often gives the playwright an opportunity to introduce ritual and stylized action in a play which ostensibly is steering away from the ritualistic."[30]

Orgel's attack on Ewbank's article appeared too late for Catherine Shaw, whose 1967 dissertation[31] covers even more territory—more than seventy plays—than Ewbank's. Shaw's basic method is, like Ewbank's, to link the masque's dramatic function and effect with the genre of the play in which it appears. But the premise behind this method—that a masque's use will be determined by the kind of play surrounding it—is too self-evident to warrant the extended discussion Shaw gives it. A revels of revenge will obviously not close a comedy, nor will a masque of reconciliation end a tragedy. Indeed, without such a predictable generic pattern to mold an audience's expectations, there would be no surprise—and little dramatic effect—in the comic ending of *The Malcontent* or the tragic ending of *The Maid's Tragedy*. The problem is that Shaw oscillates between explaining a masque by reference to the genre of the play containing it and defining a genre by reference to the kind of masque it contains. Thus in addition to comedy, tragedy, and history, Shaw gives us farce and melodrama (under melodrama we find *Antonio's Revenge*, *Valentinian*, *The Broken Heart*, *The Revenger's Tragedy*, and *Women Beware Women*). On the other hand, Shaw's commitment to a relationship between inserted masque and genre does steer her away from speculating on a relationship between the masque in drama and the Elizabethan and Jacobean court masque. To Ewbank's assertion that the masque within a play shows no clear chronological "development," we may add Shaw's conviction (suggested by Laird but here emphatically stated) that "the form of masque in Renaissance drama between 1592 and 1642 was little influenced by any further development of its sister art, the Court Masque. Rather, the type of masque utilized depended upon the service for which the dramatist intended it."[32]

After Shaw, critical focus narrows. A 1968 dissertation confines itself to Jacobean tragedy and tragicomedy[33] and distinguishes masques used as instruments of irony from masques used as analogues of the dramatic action or masques used as structural and stylistic devices.[34] A 1969 dissertation by Burton Fishman[35] concentrates on those tragedies in which the masque is fatal—especially *Antonio's Revenge*, *The Revenger's Tragedy*, and *Women Beware Women*. Fishman traces the fatal masque from Kyd's influential use of Hieronimo's play in *The Spanish Tragedy* through the simple revenge masques of Marston and Tourneur to the spectacular per-

formance in Middleton. In the process, he demolishes the remark-
ably persistent critical habit of referring to the fatal masque in
Renaissance drama as a widely used theatrical trick. He concludes:

> Since there were no more than ten fatal masques during the entire
> span of Renaissance drama, the various critical comments that speak
> of the device as an accepted cliché are perpetuating a falsehood, or, at
> least, obscuring by unguarded language what may be one of the most
> fascinating histories in drama: the creation of a convention by virtue
> of its use in an incredibly small number of plays.[36]

Much of the work done by Fishman was duplicated in an article
by M. R. Golding published several years after the dissertation
appeared.[37] Unfortunately, the published study is far less penetrat-
ing than the unpublished one. Golding observes without justification
that "it is surprising, when one considers the prevalence of a form of
the masque in Elizabethan and Jacobean plays, how little has been
written on its dramatic function."[38] Like Fishman, Golding argues
for a line of influence from Marston through Tourneur to Middleton;
like Fishman, he emphasizes the fact that only a tiny number of
revenge plays use a fatal masque. But Golding's main contention is
not found in Fishman. This is the notion that a character who uses a
masque as a cover for vengeance thereby reveals his essential
villainy. The vengeance of an Antonio or a Vindice—even of a
Hieronimo—becomes, in this view, not merely morally ambiguous
but dramatically condemned.[39] Golding writes,

> . . . it cannot be denied that there is something devious, unmanly,
> cowardly, and hence essentially villainous about the use of a masque
> to facilitate murder. How less virtuous, as a revenger, for instance,
> might Clermont be in *The Revenge of Bussy D'Ambois* had he used a
> masque, or again, what might our impression be of Hamlet had he
> stooped to this device? The implication is that dramatists became
> aware that the masque was a device appropriate only for a revenging
> villain.[40]

The application of this kind of moral yardstick to Hieronimo,
Antonio, or Vindice is, I shall argue, a preposterous response to
plays that explicitly necessitate—and then commend—a vengeance
that is "devious."

There is a set of critical terms that often appears in comments
about masques within plays and other forms of inserted entertain-

ments. Underlying these terms are several assumptions that require some attention and some cautious handling. About fifteen years ago, Lionel Abel applied the term "metatheater" to plays that, in his view, are actually about plays, or at least about the vision of life as a play.[41] A metaplay, then, is a play about itself, and (as Abel was not the first to assert) one of the several ways in which a play announces itself to be about itself is through the presence of an inserted play. Depending on which critic one is reading, the inserted play becomes the dramatist's comment on the encompassing play, or theater, or art, or life, or the relationship between reality and illusion, or all of these. A typical metacritical statement sounds like this: "Shakespeare's plays are not only about the various moral, social, political, and other thematic issues with which critics have so long and quite properly been busy but also about Shakespeare's plays."[42] The problem is that this kind of talk can lead either to a rather seductive version of the biographical fallacy or to the sort of creative criticism that John Crow called "sailing beyond the sunset."[43] The first is illustrated by two titles—*Play Within a Play: The Dramatist's Conception of His Art, Shakespeare to Anouilh* and *Drama Within Drama: Shakespeare's Sense of His Art in* King Lear, The Winter's Tale, and The Tempest[44]—that make inserted drama sound like an installment in a playwright's autobiography. Creative criticism is represented by this description of what transpires at the end of Marston's *Antonio's Revenge*: "the audience in the theater is watching an actor playing a ghost who is watching a group of characters comprising a stage audience watching a dance performed by actors who are playing specific characters who have donned masks to disguise their 'true' identities."[45] Here the critic's reading ignores the nature of theatrical convention and argues for a self-consciousness that the play simply does not urge, no matter how parodic it may be. The inserted masque has been made to provide the same kind of self-referential intrigue as Chinese boxes, the Cretan who says all Cretans are liars, or a play by Pirandello. While few studies of masques in plays treat the device solely as a direct authorial intrusion, or merely in terms that belong more properly to the theater of Tom Stoppard than to the seventeenth-century stage, both of these metacritical perspectives do appear from time to time and ought to be approached with an informed skepticism.

2

Kyd's Play, James's Masque, and London's Theaters

The Jacobean tragedies that contain masques depend for a good part of their effect upon the audience's familiarity with dramatic precursors of the device, with the nature and main components of the court masque, and with certain conditions peculiar to early seventeenth-century playhouses and acting companies. No one of these will explain or account for the inserted masque, but each is part of the essential background to the individual play. No one of the three can be called a source for the inserted masques of James's reign, but each did have a pervasive influence akin to that of a commonplace. Before embarking on a study of particular masques in particular plays, then, it would be well to recall these relevant aspects of the Renaissance theater.

The Spanish Tragedy

Kyd's play was so extraordinarily popular in its time that there can have been few London theatergoers in the first quarter of the seventeenth century who had not either seen it, read it, or heard allusions to it.[1] The play initiated a vogue, then continued to ride the crest of that vogue for some sixty years after its first performance. Its

9

insistent use of a frame and three kinds of inserted drama could hardly have passed unnoticed. Whether Kyd's frame or internal shows were specific sources for any in later drama, they do constitute a precedent of some importance. Modern critics have stressed the impact (and the interpretative problems) of Kyd's inserted play, but they have paid little attention to the masque, the dumb show, and the ways Kyd connects all of these to the omnipresent frame.[2] Those connections make Kyd's play an excellent introduction to Jacobean tragedies containing masques.

There are three intersecting planes of action in *The Spanish Tragedy*: the realm of cosmic drama represented by Don Andrea and Revenge, the realm of action in the Spanish court which is the tragedy seen by the two supernatural spectators, and the internal performance of "Soliman and Perseda." At the end of *The Spanish Tragedy*, these three—"Three parts in one, but all of discords fram'd" (3.13.173)—merge into a single "endless tragedy" (4.5.48) in the Virgilian underworld.

Don Andrea's first words reveal his supernatural identity:

> When this eternal substance of my soul
> Did live imprison'd in my wanton flesh,
> Each in their function serving other's need,
> I was a courtier in the Spanish court.
>
> (1.1.1-4)

He goes on to describe the Virgilian underworld whence he has come and to identify his companion as Revenge. Revenge's speech gives the audience its first inkling that these two characters will also be spectators:

> Then know, Andrea, that thou art arriv'd
> Where thou shalt see the author of thy death,
> Don Balthazar the prince of Portingale,
> Depriv'd of life by Bel-imperia:
> Here sit we down to see the mystery,
> And serve for Chorus in this tragedy.
>
> (1.1.86-91)

They will be part of yet apart from the play, spectators to the Spanish court but characters to Kyd's audience. That audience is now linked to the framing characters and the forthcoming "mystery" in a very special way: "Kyd's audience shares Revenge's knowledge that vengeance will come, but shares Andrea's uncertainty as to exactly how and when it will come."[3]

Revenge's words "Here sit we down to see the mystery" need further comment. First, Kyd clearly means his two supernatural spectators to remain in view throughout the play, sitting "above" or at one side of the stage.[4] Much misguided discussion of *The Spanish Tragedy*—Fredson Bowers' assertion that "the ghost has no real connection with the play,"[5] for example—has emerged from insufficient attention to the fact of their continued presence and the dramatic effects of it. Certain aspects of the final scene, for instance, are quite inexplicable without Andrea. And the fits and starts in the progress of vengeance take on considerably more significance when the theater spectators see something that readers often forget—that Revenge is asleep during a very important part of the play.

The word Revenge uses to describe the coming action—"mystery"—is an intriguing choice. It is glossed by Philip Edwards as "events with a secret meaning"; he notes that this is an uncommon usage, since "it is more usual to use the word for the secret meaning than for the events or for the story. . . . There is possibly a suggestion here of the sense 'secret rites.' "[6] Edwards rightly warns that "the word *mystery* for the old biblical plays is much later," but he too quickly concludes that "it is only a coincidence that each time Kyd uses the word, it is in the context of a stage presentation."[7] Kyd seems to be establishing a direct connection between the word "mystery," which of course also refers to the special skills of a craft or trade, and drama. Later in the play, the Spanish King reacts to the show Hieronimo presents for him with these words: "this masque contents mine eye, / Although I sound not well the mystery" (1.4.138-39). And when Andrea does not understand what the dumb show signifies, he calls "Awake, Revenge, reveal this mystery" (3.15.29). Plays, masques, and shows are mysteries throughout *The Spanish Tragedy*; the association prepares the theater audience (and should prepare the Spanish King) for the most mysterious show of all—Hieronimo's "Soliman and Perseda."

Hieronimo is established early in the play as a presenter of masques, a man who can put a performance to whatever use occasion requires with as much admirable craft as he uses in performing the marshal's duties; these are his skills, his "mysteries." He stages a

"pompous jest" (1.4.137) for the banquet honoring the Portuguese
Ambassador, then explicates it for the King and court. The "mystery" of this masque is easily explained: the three knights conquer-
ing three kings represent English victories over Portugal and Spain.
On the other hand, there is mystery still, for Andrea does not yet see
the vengeance he has been promised: "These pleasant sights are
sorrow to my soul, / Nothing but league, and love, and banqueting!"
(1.5.3-4).

Sometimes Kyd's chorus need not speak. When Isabella sees
the body of her murdered son, she naturally wants to know "the
author of this endless woe" (2.5.39). But for Kyd's audience the
"author" is not only Lorenzo but also, in another sense, Revenge,
who is interpreting the action for Andrea. Hieronimo's response to
Isabella implicitly acknowledges this: "To know the author were
some ease of grief, / For in revenge my heart would find relief"
(2.5.40-41). Isabella knows, however, that if the author of Horatio's
murder cannot immediately be found, Hieronimo will have to wait
for yet another author, the author of vengeance—time. All of this is,
to Kyd's audience, a commonplace: "The heavens are just, murder
cannot be hid, / Time is the author both of truth and right, / And time
will bring this treachery to light" (2.5.57-59). Revenge soon elabo-
rates on this familiar notion of *veritas filia temporis*: "Thou talk'st of
harvest when the corn is green: / The end is crown of every work
well done: / The sickle comes not till the corn be ripe. / Be still . . . "
(2.6.7-10).

This idea of biding one's time, waiting for *opportunitas*, is
reiterated in Hieronimo's important *Vindicta mihi* speech.[8] At this
point in the play, Hieronimo has the evidence he needs about
Horatio's murder—Bel-imperia's bloody letter has been confirmed
by Pedringano's—but the route to public retribution has been
barred by Lorenzo. The revenge must, perforce, be private:

> And to conclude, I will revenge his death!
> But how? not as the vulgar wits of men,
> With open, but inevitable ills,
> As by a secret, yet a certain mean,
> Which under kindship will be cloaked best.
>
> (3.13.20-24)

And if vengeance is private, the syllogism continues, it must be
timed:

> Wise men will take their opportunity,
> Closely and safely fitting things to time:
> But in extremes advantage hath no time,
> And therefore all times fit not for revenge.
>
> (3.13.25-28)

Finally, Hieronimo explains that the period of waiting must be spent in dissembling:

> Thus therefore will I rest me in unrest,
> Dissembling quiet in unquietness,
> Not seeming that I know their villainies,
> That my simplicity may make them think
> That ignorantly I will let all slip:
>
> (3.13.29-33)

The movement of this speech—from a recognition of divine sanction for human vengeance[9] to an understanding of the need to wait, dissembling, until the right moment for a revenge that can be cloaked in kindness—is duplicated almost step for step in the exchange between Andrea and Revenge that closes the act. The duped Andrea thinks Hieronimo is now in league with Lorenzo (3.15.15). But Revenge explains:

> Content thyself, Andrea; though I sleep,
> Yet is my mood soliciting their souls:
> Sufficeth thee that poor Hieronimo
> Cannot forget his son Horatio.
> Nor dies Revenge although he sleep awhile,
> For in unquiet, quietness is feign'd,
> And slumb'ring is a common worldly wile.
>
> (3.15.19-25)

To prove his point, Revenge presents the dumb show in which Hymen quenches the nuptial torches with blood. A placated Andrea echoes Hieronimo: "Rest thee, for I will sit to see the rest" (3.15.39).

Andrea's revenge is, of course, directed at the author of his death, Balthazar. But the revenge in the multilingual playlet is Hieronimo's for the murder of his son Horatio. This apparent discrepancy between the expectations Andrea sets up at the start of the play and the actual outcome of the tragedy has vexed many. Here, for example, is Bowers' influential summary: "the ghost of the slain

Andrea watches the revenge on the person who killed him and on those who hindered his love, but the action of the latter half of the play does not spring from the motive of a revenge for him nor is this revenge directed chiefly at his slayer."[10] Yet Kyd has taken great pains to indicate that this is not a flaw in his tragedy but a good part of its point. Andrea has set in motion the entire chain of events, a fact which is reiterated in the oft-cited image of the handkerchief and in the less often noticed references to the ransom. That ransom, promised to Horatio for the capture of Andrea's slayer Balthazar, is given to Hieronimo, who puts it to apt use:

> And as for me, my lords, I'll look to one,
> And with the ransom that the viceroy sent
> So furnish and perform this tragedy,
> As all the world shall say Hieronimo
> Was liberal in gracing of it so.
>
> (4.1.150-54)

There is also, of course, Andrea's connection with the final scenes through "those who hindered his love" for Bel-imperia, chief among whom was Castile (2.1.45-48, 3.14.111-13). Hieronimo's last act before his suicide is the murder of Castile, the offender not of Hieronimo but of Andrea. Moreover, Andrea reserves one of the most terrible punishments of the underworld for Castile (Cyprian): "Let loose poor Tityus from the vulture's gripe, / And let Don Cyprian supply his room" (4.5.31-32). Since Castile's thwarting of Andrea's love pre-dates the start of the play's action, time before the play is linked through Andrea's vengeance with the "endless tragedy" of time after the play, so that the action of *The Spanish Tragedy* is subsumed under the movement of a gripping and irrevocable cosmic drama.

Hieronimo's murder of those who took the life of his son is, like his murder of Castile, an implicit recognition of the supernatural solicitors who remain invisible to him but whose presence he indirectly acknowledges. Earlier, on finding that the author of the letter written in blood was indeed Bel-imperia, who now vows to perform the vengeance herself should he fail, Hieronimo concluded that "heaven applies our drift, / And all the saints do sit soliciting / For vengeance on those cursed murderers" (4.1.32-34).[11] The revenge had been a foregone conclusion ever since Revenge promised it to

Don Andrea at the start of the play, but the form vengeance takes proves to be Kyd's stunning contribution to the annals of inserted drama.

Several aspects of this revenge deserve repeated stress. In the first place, all avenues to public retribution have been blocked. Hieronimo cannot take his case to the marshal because he *is* the marshal, and Lorenzo has stopped his route to the King. Also, the production of "Soliman and Perseda" is made dramatically feasible by Kyd's having established Hieronimo as a presenter of shows and by providing an occasion for revels. It is the villain, not the revenger, who provides the opportunity for revenge. Both Hieronimo's on-stage audience and Kyd's theater audience know the argument of the play, so it can be performed in sundry languages "That it may breed the more variety" (4.1.174).[12] The parts of the play are so assigned that they reflect roles played in the deaths of both Horatio and Andrea. Above all, the actual means of revenge is what the Renaissance approvingly called "quaint"; it is, as Hieronimo had promised, "Not as the vulgar wits of men." Finally, the revenger dies by his own hand, so that "Revenge proves its owne Executioner."[13]

Only the very last of these does not have its rationale in the prior action, and there is ample dramatic justification for Hieronimo's suicide merely in the play's genre (though there are other good reasons for it as well). The point is that "Soliman and Perseda" is a perfectly appropriate response to the circumstances as Kyd portrays them. In this appropriateness, in the organic connection of the inserted drama with the dilemmas posed by the play, lies the significance of *The Spanish Tragedy* as a model for many of those Jacobean tragedies that contain masques.

The Court Masque

The masque of the Tudor and Stuart courts was an occasional entertainment. In James's court, masques were almost always part of the Christmas festivities, and were usually performed on or near Twelfth Night.[14] The occasion itself was invariably the honoring of some member of the royal entourage—often the sovereign though sometimes visiting royalty or betrothed aristocracy.

This honoring of royalty cannot be overemphasized, for it is the very stuff of masque. One student of the genre has written that "in all the masques performed at court, the monarch *is* the occasion, for good or for ill."[15] Another observes that "the virtue of princes is to masque as the fall of princes is to tragedy."[16] This celebration of the sovereign is reflected in every component of the masque: in the songs and the dialogue, in the scenery and the subject matter, in the elaborate preparations for performance and in the physical arrangement of the hall where the masque is given.

James watched his masques from a state in the center of the hall to which sight lines were drawn. Many an ambassadorial skirmish was fought for placement close to James, and the King did not hesitate to use spectator placement as a barometer of his political and social favor.[17] This circumstance is the basis for the exchange between Calianax and Melantius in *The Maid's Tragedy*:

> Cal.   who plac'd the Lady there
>   So neere the presence of the King?
> Mel.   I did.
> Cal.   My Lord she must not sit there.
> Mel.   Why?
> Cal.   The place is kept for women of more worth.
>   (1.2.58-61)

For Ben Jonson, masques also had a didactic purpose; they were to teach as well as to delight. "The specious hope," one critic writes with the cynicism of hindsight, is "that by telling Princes that they were perfect, they would learn to be so."[18] Yet the hope was not at all specious to Jonson, who maintained at some length and with great eloquence that masques were far more than what Bacon in 1625 dismissed as "but toys."[19] Since a number of masques in plays have a Jonsonian moralizing component, it is worth quoting his fullest statement on the subject:

> It is a noble and just advantage that the things subjected to understanding have of those which are objected to sense that the one sort are but momentary and merely taking, the other impressing and lasting. Else the glory of all these solemnities had perished like a blaze and gone out in the beholders' eyes. So short lived are the bodies of all things in comparison of their souls. And, though bodies ofttimes have the ill luck to be sensually preferred, they find afterwards the good fortune, when souls live, to be utterly forgotten. This it is hath made the most royal princes and greatest persons, who are commonly the personators of these actions, not only studious of riches and magnif-

icence in the outward celebration or show, which rightly becomes them, but curious after the most high and hearty inventions to furnish the inward parts, and those grounded upon antiquity and solid learnings; which, though their voice be taught to sound to present occasions, their sense or doth or should always lay hold on more removed mysteries. And howsoever some may squeamishly cry out that all endeavor of learning and sharpness in these transitory devices, especially where it steps beyond their little or (let me not wrong 'em) no brain at all, is superfluous, I am contented these fastidious stomachs should leave my full tables and enjoy at home their clean empty trenchers, fittest for such airy tastes, where perhaps a few Italian herbs picked up and made into a salad may find sweeter acceptance than all the most nourishing and sound meats of the world.[20]

In the courts created by the Jacobean playwrights, the makers of masques were far more likely to side with Jonson than with Bacon.

One aspect of masque that has held a particular fascination for modern critics is the nobility of the masquers. Though professional actors took the speaking parts,[21] most of a masque was performed by masked courtiers in costumes. Queen Elizabeth had been known to participate in a masque, and Henry VIII took great delight in masquery, as Shakespeare's history play shows. While James I apparently never joined a performance, his queen took roles in Daniel's *The Vision of the Twelve Goddesses* (1604) and Jonson's masques of *Blackness* (1605) and *Beauty* (1608). Prince Henry performed when heir apparent; Charles performed as heir apparent and, later, as King.

Even when King and Queen were not performing, the masque was always enacted by the court as well as for the court. This is one of the points on which the masque distinguishes itself from drama. Stephen Orgel has written that the masque

> involves its audience in ways that are impossible for the drama. Not only is it about the court it entertains, but its masquers are members of the audience, and almost always descend and join with it during the central dance, called the *revels*. The drama is properly a form of entertainment, and involves its audience vicariously. The masque is a form of play, and includes its audience directly.[22]

Characters in masques shed their fictional selves during the revels and become their literal selves. More intriguing still, in the masque proper some masquers carry *both* their fictional and real identities. This point has amazed no less a critic than Rosemond Tuve:

> . . . so astonishing it is, in fact, that I do not believe it can be under-
> stood other than historically, for in this pure form it flourished and
> died with the court masque. One can think of no other genre that
> exhibits it, and pleasure in it is a learned response.
>   Certain ones of the characters are not characters but masquers;
> they are not court personages *acting* parts in a play, but have, as
> themselves, been written into a dramatic piece, and play in it without
> ceasing to be themselves.[23]

It is indeed a complex point for the twentieth century (how can we
know the masquer from the masque?), but for the sixteenth and
seventeenth centuries it was a rich but quite conventional conceit,
fascinating not so much in itself as for what could be made of it in an
evening's entertainment at court—or within the confines of a play in
one of London's theaters.

There is a final point to be made about the conditions of a
masque's performance. When critics observe the pronounced difference between the golden and decorous world of some masques
within plays and the violent or comic action of the play proper, they
are noticing something that was occasionally also the case at James's
court. Cyrus Hoy has found in this an example of mannerism:

> The spectacle of a court whose moral tone was not high witnessing
> and enacting the grave and learned and indeed often sublime philo-
> sophic fables which Jonson provided for its ritual occasions brings
> sharply into focus the tension between spiritualism and sensualism,
> rationalism and irrationalism, which is at the heart of the crisis of the
> Renaissance, and of the mannerist style.[24]

Hoy's idea is certainly attractive, and there is much in what he says
that invites comparison with mannerism in art. On the other hand, it
is unlikely that Sir John Harington thought he was pondering the
crisis of the Renaissance when he wrote this account of a masque
given in 1606 for Queen Anne's brother, Christian IV of Denmark:

> One day, a great feast was held, and, after dinner, the representation
> of Soloman his Temple and the coming of the Queen of Sheba was
> made, or (as I may better say) was meant to have been made, before
> their Majesties, by device of the Earl of Salisbury and others. But
> alass! as all earthly thinges do fail to poor mortals in enjoyment, so did
> prove our presentment hereof. The Lady who did play the Queens
> part, did carry most precious gifts to both their Majesties; but, forget-
> ting the steppes arising to the canopy, overset her caskets into his

Danish Majesties lap, and fell at his feet, tho I rather think it was in
his face. Much was the hurry and confusion; cloths and napkins were
at hand, to make all clean. His Majesty then got up and would dance
with the Queen of Sheba; but he fell down and humbled himself
before her, and was carried to an inner chamber, and laid on a bed of
state; which was not a little defiled with the presents of the Queen
which had been bestowed on his garments; such as wine, cream, jelly,
beverage, cakes, spices, and other good matters. The entertainment
and show went forward, and most of the presenters went backward,
or fell down; wine did so occupy their upper chambers. Now did
appear, in rich dress, Hope, Faith, and Charity: Hope did assay to
speak, but wine rendered her endeavors so feeble that she withdrew,
and hoped the King would excuse her brevity: Faith was then all
alone, for I am certain she was not joyned with good works, and left
the court in a staggering condition: Charity came to the King's feet,
and seemed to cover the multitude of sins her sisters had committed; in
some sorte she made obeysance and brought giftes, but said she would
return home again, as there was no gift which heaven had not already
given his Majesty. She then returned to Hope and Faith, who were
both sick and spewing in the lower hall.[25]

Harington's account, like the revelry, goes on. While this kind of
thing probably did not happen often, it does suggest that decorum
sometimes went quite athwart in life as well as in art.

The matter of masques resembles drama no more than does its
manner. Instead of dramatic plots or stories, masques have hinges,
arguments, inventions, or central conceits. Here, for example, is
Jonson's explanation of the argument of his last court masque
Chloridia (1631), the ending of which was later satirized in his
"Expostulation with Inigo Jones":

> . . . it was agreed that it should be the celebration of some rites done to
> the goddess Chloris, who in a general council of the gods was pro-
> claimed goddess of the flowers, according to that of Ovid in the
> *Fasti*: *Arbitrium tu, dea, floris habe*. And was to be stellified on earth
> by an absolute decree from Jupiter, who would have the earth to be
> adorned with stars, as well as the heaven.
>
> (4-10).

"Upon this hinge," Jonson adds, "the whole invention moved."

The elements of masque that serve the hinge are words, music,
scenery, and dancing, all of which are suffused with symbolism,
imagery, iconography, emblems, and allegory. Different elements
have their champions: to Jonson the poetry was the soul of masque,

while to Jones the architectural trappings were all.[26] Even Jonson, however, occasionally sighed for the whole that was far more than the sum of its parts: "Only the envy was that it lasted not still, or, now it is past, cannot by imagination, much less description, be recovered to a part of that spirit it had in the gliding by" (*Hymenaei*, 529-32). We risk much, then, if we say that any one element is masque's *raison d'etre*. There is, however, a consistent theme in the critical literature: "All the evidence shows that the predominant feature of the early masque was dancing, and it is with dancing that Shakespeare always associates it."[27] The masque is "not primarily a drama; it is an episode in an indoor revel of dancing."[28] From Stephen Orgel, who has devoted a career to the language of masques, we learn that "most of a masque was not literature."[29] "The nucleus around which the Mask, as a dramatic genre, was constructed was dance, and can fairly be described as choreographic compliment."[30] Finally, "but perhaps each overestimated the importance of his contribution—Jonson his fable and Jones his scenic designs, for the chief element of this form of entertainment, even in the earliest accounts, was dancing."[31] It is at least possible that, Ben Jonson notwithstanding, the Jacobean theater audiences aligned masque more closely with dancing than with either the poetry or the scene. Certainly the Jacobean playwright did not hesitate to let a character call "masque" that which was nothing more than revels.

The format of masque was standardized fairly early in James's reign. With Jonson's introduction of the antimasque in 1608, there emerged a fairly consistent pattern to the Stuart masque. The antimasque comes first, followed by the discovery—to loud music— of the scene for the masque proper and the first song. A presenter then announces the masquers, who dance their entry. After a second song, the masquers descend from the stage for a third song and the revels, in which both masquers and spectators participate. At the end of the evening, there is a fourth song and a final dance by the masquers.[32] Though this outline is of course too general to cover every masque, it does indicate the norm from which variations were made both at court and in plays.

A few components that are regularly seen in seventeenth-century plays deserve emphasis. The antimasque was Jonson's contribution, but it was not entirely his invention and he does not seem to regard it as such. He simply appropriated the Tudor antic

masque—a grotesque, disorderly, and antic dance that embodied the
concept of "misrule"—and placed it before the main masque (hence
sometimes "antemasque") as a foil or parodic "antimasque." Here is
his gloss on *Queens* (with a reference to the *Haddington Masque* of
the previous year):

> And because her majesty (best knowing that a principal part of life in
> these spectacles lay in their variety) had commanded me to think on
> some dance or show that might precede hers and have the place of a
> foil or false masque, I was careful to decline not only from others', but
> mine own steps in that kind, since the last year I had an antimasque of
> boys; and therefore now devised that twelve women in the habit of
> hags or witches, sustaining the persons of Ignorance, Suspicion,
> Credulity, etc., the opposites to good Fame, should fill that part, not
> as a masque but a spectacle of strangeness, producing multiplicity of
> gesture, and not unaptly sorting with the current and whole fall of the
> device.
>
> (8-19)

The antimasque in *Queens* is the masque's opposite in every respect: in the discordance of its language and songs, in the purpose of
its principal masquer—"To overthrow the glory of this night"
(101)—and in its dance "full of preposterous change and gesticulation" (328) that travesties both the masquers' dance and the revels.
When much the same kind of "spectacle of strangeness" appeared in
Jacobean plays like *The Duchess of Malfi* and *The Changeling*, the
links to both the Elizabethan antic masque and the more recent
Jacobean antimasque could not but be noted by early audiences.

The loud music so often associated with masques was more than
accompaniment to songs and dances. Jonson notes that when Fame
appeared in *Queens*, the music "waited on the turning" (429) of the
machina versatilis. Andrew Sabol has explained that "after the
antimasquers' song and dance, the accounts frequently refer to 'a
loud music,' apparently played with sufficient majesty not only to
usher in the grand pageant of the elaborately costumed masquers,
but also to cover up the noise made by creaking stage machinery."[33]
Music also filled gaps in the action, as when "the loud music sounded
as before, to give the masquers time of descending" (*Queens*,
447-48). But it is mainly as a cover for noise that music served the
masqued characters of tragedy: "And therefore, in the height of all
the revels, / When music was heard loudest, courtiers busiest, / And

ladies great with laughter—O, vicious minute" (*The Revenger's Tragedy*, 1.4.37-39).

The presenter is another feature of masques that often served dramatists. In *Queens*, Heroic Virtue bridges the gap between anti-masque and masque by presenting the queens directly to James, "To you, most royal and most happy king, / Of whom Fame's house in every part doth ring / For every virtue . . ." (408-10). In a number of plays, most notably perhaps *The Duchess of Malfi*, a character "presents" in a way that is recognizably analogous to the way Heroic Virtue and other presenters function in the Jacobean court masque.

The culmination—though not yet the close—of masque is the revels. While the dances of the revels come after what we normally call the masque proper, they remain within the frame, as it were, of the evening's entertainment. That entire entertainment, not merely the part of it that takes place on stage, is the masque. The final dance and song of the masquers takes place *after* the revels, enclosing the spectators, who dance in the revels, *within* the whole invention or device. This fact too has interested Rosemond Tuve, who writes:

> The evening ball ('revels') is of course normally enclosed within the masque proper, with the final speeches kept until, after the listeners' dancing, they close at once both the action and the evening. Since a masque always honors someone, this particular unity of participating groups, one 'assisting' as at a ritual, bears resemblance to something we know chiefly in services of worship.[34]

Tuve's analogy is not at all far-fetched: James I was, after all, the first English monarch to insist on the absolute Divine Right of Kings. Yet here again we forget at our peril that what is all but foreign to the twentieth century was convention in the seventeenth. But precisely because it was convention, the masque—that curious genre that so intrigues Tuve, that so engaged Jonson and Jones and so flattered James—proved a particularly flexible and useful device for some of the best playwrights of the age.

Some of the best playwrights of the age themselves wrote masques. Marston contributed *The Entertainment at Ashby* (1607), Beaumont wrote *The Masque of the Inner Temple and Gray's Inn* (1613), Middleton wrote the lost *Masque of Cupid* (1614), *The Inner Temple Masque, or Masque of Heroes* (1619), and, in collaboration with Rowley, *The World Tossed at Tennis* (1620).[35] What relationships may exist between these masques and those in plays written by their authors is a subject best relegated to treatment of individual plays. But since the present discussion of the court masque has emphasized what the Jacobean theater audience would understand to be the features of the genre, it seems appropriate to observe that most of the playwrights who admitted masques to their plays knew firsthand whereof they wrote.

The Boy Companies and the Second Blackfriars

Aspects of the inserted masque that are not accounted for by reference to the precedent set in *The Spanish Tragedy* or the fashion for masques at court are often traced to two developments in the early seventeenth-century theater. One of these is the great vogue enjoyed by the boy companies during the first decade of the century; the other is the appearance of adult companies in private theaters after 1609, when the King's Men acquired the second Blackfriars for their winter home.

Most of the plays containing masques that were first performed between 1599 and 1611 are found in the repertories of the children's troupes. The Children of Paul's acted *Antonio and Mellida* and *Antonio's Revenge* (both 1599–1600), *Satiromastix* (1601), *Blurt, Master Constable* (1601–02), *The Fawn* (c. 1604), and *A Mad World, My Masters* (1604–06). The list of plays containing masques acted by the Children of the Chapel Royal (also known as the Children of the Queen's Revels and the Children of the Blackfriars) during the same period includes *Cynthia's Revels* (1600), *May Day* (1601–02), *The Gentleman Usher* (1602–03), *The Malcontent* (c. 1603), *The Dutch Courtesan* (1603–05), *The Fawn* (c. 1604), *Your Five Gallants* (1604–07), *The Widow's Tears* (c. 1605), *Sophonisba* (1605–06), *The Tragedy of Byron* (1608), and *The Insatiate Countess* (1609–11).[36] Although there are masques in the King's Men's *The Revenger's Tragedy* and *Timon of Athens*, the association between very full inserted masques and plays acted by boys is not broken until late 1610 or early 1611 when the King's Men performed Beaumont and Fletcher's *The Maid's Tragedy* at Blackfriars. By late 1610, however, the Children of Paul's had been inactive for four years and the Children of Blackfriars were all but silent.

There is no single or simple explanation for this association. One certain factor is that plays written for boys were replete with songs and music, and many of those musical pieces accompanied inserted masques. The boys who formed the original Elizabethan troupes were Cathedral and Royal Chapel choristers, and although some members of the Jacobean companies were not choirboys, the plays continued to be riddled with music. Michael Shapiro has calculated that

> After the late 1590s, 16 of the 21 plays (76%) acted by the Children of Paul's contain a total of 80 songs, or an average of 5 each, while 72% of the plays acted by the Chapel Children contain an average of 2.4 songs per play. By comparison, only 49% of the plays acted by Shakespeare's troupe during a corresponding period contain songs; the average of 1.4 songs per play is considerably lower than that for the plays acted by children's troupes, and plays acted by other adult troupes contain even fewer songs.[37]

A number of the songs in plays performed by boys introduce or form part of a masque; in *Antonio and Mellida*, for example, no fewer than three songs precede the entrance of Galeatzo and his fellow masquers.[38] On the other hand, there was nothing about the masque itself—as distinguished from the songs before or after it—that could not be handled quite well by "Malevole in folio": Marston's *The Malcontent*, first written for boys at Blackfriars, was acted by the King's Men at the Globe with its masque intact but without "the not-received custom of music in our theater."[39]

The group of dramatists writing for the children's troupes in the first decade of the seventeenth century was quite small. Of those responsible for the bulk of these plays—Jonson, Chapman, Marston, and Middleton—the first was already deeply committed to the court masque and the other three were to produce major masques during James's reign.[40] It may be, then, that the abundance of masques in boys' plays feeds a playwright's penchant for the genre as much as it indulges the boys' musical talents.

There may also be an occasional connection between an inserted masque and the peculiar license enjoyed by the boy companies. The boys could mock, satirize, and abuse where the adult players dared not; as Rosencrantz observed of the children's theaters, "many wearing rapiers are afraid of goosequills and dare scarce come thither" (*Ham.*, 2.2.336-37). A good deal of this vituperation was directed at the court, and one aspect of the court that was easily satirized was its devotion to masques. In due course the children's license to abuse was itself abused; more than one playwright went to prison for striking too close to home. The French Ambassador to James's court, Boderie, gave this account of his reaction to a play by Chapman:

> I caused certain players to be forbid from acting the history of the Duke of Byron; when, however, they saw that the whole Court had left the town, they persisted in acting it; nay, they brought upon the stage the Queen of France and Mademoiselle de Verneuil. The former, having accosted the latter with very hard words, gave her a box on the ear. At my suit, three of them were arrested, but the principal person, the author, escaped.[41]

The scene Boderie describes must have been expunged by the censor, for there is no such quarrel in *Byron* and Chapman speaks in the dedication of "these poor dismembered poems." The intriguing thing is that there remains a masque clearly pertaining to the excised quarrel scene.[42] After watching this masque, Henry IV says, "This show hath pleased me well for that it figures / The reconcilement of my Queen and mistress" (2.1.128-29), but there is no such reconcilement in the play either. It is possible, though obviously difficult to substantiate, that in this and some of the other plays performed by boys, the court-baiting element suggested inclusion of a masque.

Contributing much more to the frequent appearance of masques in early seventeenth-century plays were the theaters in which the boys, and later the adults, played, and the kind of audience those theaters attracted. One particularly important playhouse was the second Blackfriars, home from 1600 to the Children of the Chapel Royal and, after 1609, the winter playhouse of the King's Men.

The major differences between a private theater such as the Blackfriars and a public theater such as the Globe are well known and need be only briefly recalled here. Public playhouses were large, unroofed amphitheaters holding as many as three thousand spectators. The lowest admission fee bought standing room near the stage; higher prices were charged for seats in the galleries. Private theaters were enclosed, artificially lit, and much smaller, holding perhaps five or six hundred seated spectators. Those closest to the stage paid more than those in the galleries—reversing the Globe's priorities—and even the cheapest admission was six times the lowest price at a public playhouse.[43] The private theater's audience tended naturally to come from the aristocracy and the professional classes; they were "actual, potential, or self-styled figures of power and responsibility who wanted and could afford vicarious participation in a courtly occasion."[44] It is readily apparent that the conditions of the Blackfriars and the tastes of its audience were a spawning ground for masques. Almost all of those plays with masques approaching the scale of masques at court (such as *Cynthia's Revels*, *The Tragedy of Byron*, *The Maid's Tragedy*, and *The Tempest*) seem to have been first performed in private theaters, or halls at court, where the scenes and machines associated with court masques could be handled.

Yet the very real differences between public and private theaters should not blind us to the adaptability of Jacobean playwrights and players. *The Malcontent* was, as we have seen, taken over by the King's Men masque and all, and there is not a shred of evidence to support the suggestion that "when *The Maid's Tragedy* . . . was performed in the public theater the masque was omitted."[45] While the private theater certainly encouraged the incursion of masque, at no point did it become masque's sole proprietor.

Kyd's play, James's masque, and London's theaters: these are the factors most often cited as contributing to the appearance of masques within plays.[46] The masque appeared in plays because Kyd showed what could be done with interior shows; the masque appeared in plays because it was appearing at court; the masque appeared in plays because theatrical conditions made its appearance possible. Much seems explained, yet really very little has been. We have, so to speak, the gloss but not the text. There remains the final cause, that for the sake of which: the individual play. In the final analysis, nothing accounts for a masque in a play quite so well as the play in which it appears.

3

Marston's *Antonio's Revenge*

Antonio's Revenge is only half the title of John Marston's first tragedy. The other half, as given on the title page of the 1602 quarto, is *The second part*. The first part is, of course, *The History of Antonio and Mellida. The first part.* To stress the full titles of these plays is not merely to quibble over something that Marston himself may not have controlled, but to suggest that most members of an audience to the second part had at least a passing acquaintance with the first part. Performed by the same company[1] within the same year,[2] Marston's two Antonio plays, while almost certainly never played back to back at a single performance, do form one two-part play. The action through the ten acts is continuous, and there are promises in the first part of a sequel as well as references in the second part to incidents in the first. Even allowing for the chance that allusions to the companion piece were standard poetical posturing or a conventional mode of advertising, the two plays do complement each other in a host of ways. As the editor of the Regents edition has observed, "the relationship of the two parts of *Antonio and Mellida* depends upon a series of parallel yet contrasting incidents, set against one another, act against act."[3] A noteworthy instance of this relationship is the appearance in the second part of an event that figures significantly in the first part: a nuptial masque. The dramatic power of the masque sequence in *Antonio's Revenge* is therefore enriched—for Marston's first audiences as well as his modern readers—by familiarity with certain anticipatory incidents in *Antonio and Mellida*.

The curious Induction that opens *Antonio and Mellida* includes a notice of (or at least a trial balloon suggesting) a second part. The actor who is to play Antonio announces that "I have heard that those persons, as he and you, Feliche, that are but slightly drawn in this comedy, should receive more exact accomplishment in a second part; which, if this obtain gracious acceptance, means to try his fortune" (Induction, 134-38). The rumor will prove less than accurate: the "he" mentioned here is Galeatzo, who appears very late in *Antonio's Revenge* and who receives less "accomplishment" there than in *Antonio and Mellida*. Feliche is killed off between the two plays and is replaced in the second by his father, Pandulpho.[4] The playwright is naturally entitled to change his plans, or to thwart the expectations of his audience, but Marston's serving notice of a sequel so early in the first play would, at the very least, pique the curiosity of many spectators.

The Induction is followed by a cheery Prologue that is then sharply juxtaposed to Antonio's bleak opening speech. The Prologue invokes "The wreath of pleasure, and delicious sweets" (1) and promises the assembly not "bended brow, but dimpled smiles" (23). The soliloquy that follows, however, is so laden with bended brow that it could be plucked from *Antonio and Mellida* and inserted nearly whole into almost any scene in *Antonio's Revenge*. The especially anticipatory final lines are set off and stressed by cornets that sound Piero's flourish and sennet as if they were punctuation for Antonio's words:

> Hark how Piero's triumphs beat the air.
> O rugged mischief, how thou grat'st my heart!
> Take spirit, blood; disguise, be confident;
> Make a firm stand; here rests the hope of all:
> Lower than hell there is no depth to fall.
>
> (1.1.30-34)

Many of these words will be heard again in both plays: "triumphs," "disguise," "hell," "fall." The word most iterative in *Antonio's Revenge*, though, is "mischief." The association here introduced between mischief and Piero's deeds is a link that runs right through the tragedy in Piero's words and actions as well as in the language of

Antonio's reactions. Ultimately, mischief is what Antonio himself must wreak in order to gain his revenge. The word was, we should remember, far stronger in Marston's day than in our own.[5] When, to cite a well-known example, Shakespeare's Antony is left alone in the Forum after reading Caesar's will, he says "Now let it work. Mischief, thou art afoot, / Take thou what course thou wilt" (*JC*, 3.2.260-61). In Marston's comedy, Piero's strutting and his courtiers' fawning give Feliche cause to wish "Confusion to these limber sycophants! / No sooner mischief's born in regenty / But flattery christens it with 'policy'" (1.1.74-76). Piero, however, has other plans: "Pish! I prosecute my family's revenge, / Which I'll pursue with such a burning chase / Till I have dried up all Andrugio's blood" (1.1.87-89). Though he can dry no blood in the comedy, Piero will come very close to making good on the promise in the sequel.

   The second act of *Antonio and Mellida*, which ends with far more hope for the young lovers than did the first, is shot through with music and dance. There is "the descant you made upon our names" (2.1.45-46) sung by Catzo and Dildo (the lyrics are, alas, lost) and a dance in honor of Piero's victories. While this dance sequence is evidently not a masque, it does anticipate the masque at the end of the play. From his state Piero exhorts Mellida to "Look sprightly" (2.1.156) while three groups of dancers tread their measures (2.1.151.3-6). Mellida's apostrophe to music is both a conventional nod to decorum and a lyrical reaction to the reported loss of Antonio:

> Come, come, let's dance. O music, thou distill'st
> More sweetness in us than this jarring world;
> Both time and measure from thy strains do breathe,
> Whilst from the channel of this dirt doth flow
> Nothing but timeless grief, unmeasured woe.
>   (2.1.191-95)

But the sentiment is undercut both by the disguised Antonio's indecorous fall (2.1.201) and by the easy banter between Piero's gentlemen and their ladies. Piero ends the dance with the conventional call for lights and drink: "Fill out Greek wines; prepare fresh cressetlight; / We'll have a banquet, princes, then good night" (2.1.254-55).

   The third act is an interlude of reactions: Andrugio's reaction to his defeat, Feliche's reaction to the "nocturnal court delights" (3.2.6) and to those who indulge in them, Piero's reaction to Mellida's

escape, Antonio's reaction to Piero's discovery. Confusion triumphs—
"Backward and forward, every way about" (3.2.264)—and Feliche
has the last word: "I hate not man, but man's lewd qualities"
(3.2.276).

Preparations for Mellida's forced marriage to Galeatzo begin in
the fourth act. Before she is found, however, there is an ominous
exchange between Andrugio and Antonio. Responding to his father's embrace, Antonio says,

> Bless not the body with your twining arms
> Which is accurst of heaven. O, what black sin
> Hath been committed by our ancient house,
> Whose scalding vengeance lights upon our heads,
> That thus the world and fortune casts us out
> As loathed objects, Ruin's branded slaves.
>
> (4.1.118-23)

Andrugio's answer is simple: "Do not expostulate the heavens'
will." Both the complaint and the response are certainly germane to
this scene, but they also introduce a vision of divine vengeance that
is assimilated into *Antonio's Revenge*, and that might well color a
spectator's reaction to the happy ending of the comedy by anticipat-
ing the events of the tragedy.

When Mellida is found at last, Piero orders an immediate
marriage: "Young prince, mount up your spirits and prepare / To
solemnize your nuptial's eve with pomp" (4.1.260-61). Galeatzo
agrees: "The time is scant; now nimble wits appear; / Phoebus
begins to gleam, the welkin's clear" (4.1.262-63). Though neither
Piero nor Galeatzo mentions it by name, Balurdo takes the call for
"nimble wits" as a summons for a masque. He makes hasty plans to
"mount my courser and most gallantly prick," to "speak pure
rhyme," and to "tickle the Muses" (4.1.268, 271, 276-77), all of
which is met with more than a little skepticism from Dildo ("Balurdo,
thou art an arrant sot"). Shortly thereafter, Balurdo is seen exhorting
a painter to draw him a device: "a good fat leg of ewe mutton
swimming in stew'd broth of plums," or "a driveling, reeling song,
and let the word be, 'Uh,'" or—finally—"a good massy ring with
your own posy graven in it" (5.1.20-21, 27-28, 32-33). He also gives
Feliche an extended description of what he intends to wear in the
masque; Feliche finds this quite tedious but will, like Marston's

audience, recognize Balurdo at once when the masquers enter. It is an elaborate catalogue, and probably not representative—Balurdo being Balurdo—of what Galeatzo and Matzagente might wear:

> If you see one in a yellow taffeta doublet cut upon carnation velour, a green hat, a blue pair of velvet hose, a gilt rapier and an orange-tawny pair of worsted silk stockings, that's I. . . . I ha' bought me a new green feather with a red sprig; you shall see my wrought shirt hang out at my breeches; you shall know me.
>
> (5.1.77-79, 82-84)

And in his parting shot, Balurdo confirms what Marston's audience surely suspected—that Balurdo plans to grace (or disgrace) Mellida's nuptial masque: "Marry, in the masque 'twill be somewhat hard. But if you hear anybody speak so wittily that he makes all the room laugh, that's I, that's I" (5.1.86-88).

The long and busy final scene of *Antonio and Mellida* is a series of shows. There is a singing contest, an entry of masquers followed by revels, and two spectacular revelations that, while not part of the masque proper, act as a great Jonsonian double "hinge" in resolving discord into peace.

The scene opens with Piero's call to revelry: "Advance the music's prize; now cap'ring wits / Rise to your highest mount; let choice delight / Garland the brow of this triumphant night" (5.2.1-3). One of the court's particularly capering wits, Forobosco, demolishes that dignified summons in a line ("'Sfoot, 'a sits like Lucifer himself") and so sets a pattern for the scene. Two apparently acceptable songs are performed by boys vying for the gilt harp but both are mocked out of the contest by Rossaline, who dubs Balurdo victor and knight of the golden harp (5.2.28). It is an honor he will recall frequently in *Antonio's Revenge*. Rossaline continues in this spirited vein with a good-humored diatribe against men and marriage, while Piero briefly plays straight man. When the masquers enter, Piero calls for room and—as he has done once before—urges his daughter to dance.[6] There are, again, three sets of dancers: Mellida reads the device of Galeatzo, Rossaline reads the device of Matzagente, and Flavia reads the device of Balurdo. Each of the three exchanges ends with the lady making light of the courtier's high seriousness (or, in Balurdo's case, low seriousness). Just as Balurdo is (figuratively) trussing his codpiece point (5.2.125), a flourish halts the revels.

Feliche's comment on arriving at the masque shows typical disdain for the conventions of the court: "Stand away. Here's such a company of flyboats hulling about this galleas of greatness that there's no boarding him" (5.2.127-28). He manages nonetheless to present to Piero a knight who "hath brought Andrugio's head" (5.2.131). The presenting and unmasking of Andrugio and Antonio unfold in the manner of a masque. Both are discoveries that amaze and astonish the on-stage spectators (5.2.166-67, 218-20) as well as Marston's theater audience. The entry of Lucio with Antonio's coffin is called a "tragic spectacle" (173), and Antonio himself says, "There stands my tomb and here a pleasing stage, / Most wish'd spectators of my tragedy" (214-15). But tragedy is cast aside, and the promise of the Prologue fulfilled, when Piero honors his vows, welcomes Andrugio, and gives his consent to the marriage of Mellida and Antonio. The "nimble wits" whom Galeatzo called to the masque are Andrugio and Antonio, for after they unmask, "Now there remains no discord that can sound / Harsh accents to the ear of our accord" (251-52). The ending is all comedy as Piero calls for music: "Sound Lydian wires; once make a pleasing note / On nectar streams of your sweet airs to float" (262-63).

The nuptial masque that gives occasion to reconciliation in *Antonio and Mellida* is the occasion for vengeance in *Antonio's Revenge*. Yet the masque is not quite the simple "parallel yet contrasting incident" G. K. Hunter sees as a link between the plays. Though the two masques lead to starkly different ends, and therefore do stand in the neat juxtaposition that critics are fond of observing, they also share at least one important effect: each resolves discord, confusion, and (to use Marston's term) mischief through a process of unmasking that intrudes itself into the planned but aborted nuptial revels. Attention to this process, and to the several actions and reactions that lead up to it, belies the common view that the masque in *Antonio's Revenge* is merely token or conventional and underscores those circumstances that lead inexorably toward the manner of Antonio's revenge.

The opening soliloquy in *Antonio's Revenge*, unlike that in *Antonio and Mellida*, confirms most emphatically the promise of the Prologue. The spectator who does not seek "a sullen tragic scene," "Who winks and shuts his apprehension up / From common sense of what men were, and are, / Who would not know what men must be" is warned to "Hurry amain from our black-visaged shows" (Prologue, 7, 17-19, 20). The stunning entrance that follows is an emblem of that "sullen tragic scene" and its motto is Piero's own:

> "One. Two." Lord, in two hours what a topless mount
> Of unpeered mischief have these hands cast up!
> I can scarce coop triumphing Vengeance up
> From bursting forth in braggart passion.
>
>   (1.1.9-12)

The audience is not long kept in suspense:

> Andrugio sleeps in peace! this brain hath choked
> The organ of his breast. Feliche hangs
> But as a bait upon the line of death
> To 'tice on mischief. I am great in blood,
> Unequaled in revenge.
>
>   (1.1.14-18)

The association between mischief and vengeance is struck and held from this first scene to the last. Both words are quickly glossed: "mischief" in the passage just cited, and "vengeance" in this explanation:

> We both were rivals in our May of blood
> Unto Maria, fair Ferrara's heir.
> He won the Lady, to my honour's death,
> And from her sweets cropped this Antonio;
> For which I burned in inward swelt'ring hate,
> And festered rankling malice in my breast,
> Till I might belk revenge upon his eyes.
>
>   (1.1.23-29)

What is noteworthy here is not so much that Marston has contrived a motivation for Piero—Marston never shows much interest in motivation[7]—as that this justification is quite different from the one Antonio is now able to make. This is vengeance not for the death of blood kin but for the death of "honour." Moreover, this is vengeance taken not as a public action worthy of defense, but as a secret and Italianate act:

> That I should drop strong poison in the bowl
> Which I myself caroused unto his health
> And future fortune of our unity;

> That it should work even in the hush of night,
> And strangle him on sudden, that fair show
> Of death for the excessive joy of his fate
> Might choke the murder! Ha, Strotzo, is't not rare?
> Nay, but weigh it—then Feliche stabbed
> (Whose sinking thought frighted my conscious heart)
> And laid by Mellida, to stop the match
> And hale on mischief. This all in one night!
>
> (1.1.68-78)

Andrugio is poisoned, Feliche stabbed, and Mellida about to be dishonored; each deed has been done with mischief in the name of vengeance. Piero is made to belabor these details not merely for Strotzo's benefit or to vent his own "braggart passion"; he pauses over them also, I think, so that Marston's audience has a foil for Antonio's reactions and the mischiefs yet to come.

By the end of the first act, all three deeds have been discovered. Antonio's reactions are the key ones: when the curtain is drawn to reveal Feliche's body, Antonio finds the spectacle an affront to Mellida, and when Piero proclaims Mellida's chastity tainted, Antonio is stayed from instant vengeance only by his mother's hand. But Andrugio's death carries as yet no trace of suspicion. Antonio, who has seen bleeding ghosts in his dream and a blazing comet out his window (1.3.39-56), knows something is amiss: "Why now the womb of mischief is delivered / Of the prodigious issue of the night" (1.5.24-25). Lacking cause to act, though, he can only react: "Are thy moist entrails crumpled up with grief / Of parching mischief?" (1.5.43-44), and a little later, apostrophizing woe, "If there be any horror yet unfelt, / Unthought of mischief in thy fiendlike power, / Dash it upon my miserable head" (1.5.52-54).

The end of the first act and all of the second continue the triumph of Piero's mischiefs while measuring Antonio's despair against the stoical laughter and defiance of Pandulpho, the admonition *"Ferte fortiter"* that Antonio reads in Seneca (2.3.45), and the grief of Maria and Mellida. In a watershed passage that marks the apex of his woe, Antonio claims the prize: "Behold a prostrate wretch laid on his tomb; / His epitaph thus: *Ne plus ultra*. Ho! / Let none out-woe me, mine's Herculean woe" (2.3.131-133). Piero, meanwhile, stands at the apex of his mischief:

> Swell plump, bold heart,

For now thy tide of vengeance rolleth in.
O now *Tragoedia Cothurnata* mounts;
Piero's thoughts are fixed on dire exploits;
Pell mell! Confusion and black murder guides
The organs of my spirit—

(2.5.43-48)

But from this moment on, the tide of vengeance turns; Antonio
begins to act. The change is caused by the ghost of his father, marked
by the movement of Piero's iterative words "vengeance" and "mischief" into Antonio's lines, and ended only by the return of mischief
for mischief, blood for blood, vengeance for vengeance. The text for
all that ensues is contained in a single speech, in the charge made by
Andrugio's Ghost to Antonio:

Antonio, revenge!
I was empoisoned by Piero's hand;
Revenge my blood!—take spirit, gentle boy—
Revenge my blood! Thy Mellida is chaste;
Only to frustrate thy pursuit in love
Is blazed unchaste. Thy mother yields consent
To be his wife and give his blood a son,
That made her husbandless and doth complot
To make her sonless. But before I touch
The banks of rest, my ghost shall visit her.
Thou vigour of my youth, juice of my love,
Seize on revenge, grasp the stern-bended front
Of frowning vengeance with unpeisèd clutch.
Alarum Nemesis, rouse up thy blood,
Invent some stratagem of vengeance
Which, but to think on, may like lightning glide
With horror through thy breast. Remember this:
Scelera non ulcisceris, nisi vincis.

(3.1.34-51)

The Senecan tag, lifted from Atreus' first speech in *Thyestes*, is the
crux of both the speech and the scene, the epigraph to the masque
and perhaps to the entire play. The notion that wrong is avenged
only when conquered or surpassed is the guide to Antonio's actions
from this point on. In linking the manner of Antonio's revenge with
the manner of Piero's mischiefs, it is the gloss on the mischief that
henceforth stems less from Piero than from Antonio. That Antonio
takes the Ghost's charge to heart is clear from his conflation of two
passages uttered by Seneca's Ghost of Tantalus, to which Antonio

appends the word *"Ulciscar"* (3.2.15-22), and from the English vow
that follows:

> May I be cursèd by my father's ghost
> And blasted with incensèd breath of heaven,
> If my heart beat on ought but vengeance.
> May I be numbed with horror and my veins
> Pucker with singeing torture, if my brain
> Digest a thought, but of dire vengeance;
> May I be fettered slave to coward chance,
> If blood, heart, brain, plot ought save vengeance!
>
> (3.2.34-41)

Antonio has an opportunity to "suck red vengeance / Out of
Piero's wounds" (3.2.78-79) very soon after his vow is made. But he
lets it slip (3.2.87.1-2) for a most significant reason: "No, not so, /
This shall be sought for; I'll force him feed on life / Till he shall loathe
it. This shall be the close / Of vengeance' strain" (3.2.88-91). This is a
view of vengeance common in plays ending with a revels of revenge
and in plays where the revenger explicitly rejects that vengeance
which takes its victim asleep or at prayer; the notion is invoked in
varying contexts in *Hamlet* (3.3.73-96), *The Revenger's Tragedy*
(especially 2.2.89-93, 127; 2.3.3-4, 10-14), *The Maid's Tragedy*
(5.1.24-35), *The Duchess of Malfi* (5.4.44-45), and *Women Beware
Women* (5.2.24-29). Underlying all these is the conviction that
murder only takes on the sanction of vengeance when, in due course
of time, "the wicked is snared in the worke of his owne hands"
(Psalms 9:16).[8] Antonio's lines are not only the rationale for his
present inaction; they are also profoundly anticipatory of the revenge that finally does come: "the close / Of vengeance' strain"
looks forward to the masque's measure and its closing song, while
"I'll force him feed on life / Till he shall loathe it" is a metaphor
stunningly literalized in the dish served up to Piero at the banquet of
revenge.

As false occasion is properly rejected when Antonio lets Piero
live, so true occasion is properly seized when Antonio has Julio die.
The distinctions between the two opportunities are underscored by
Antonio's recognition at the second one of heaven's justice (3.3.6), by
his Senecan tag (3.3.7-8),[9] and especially by the apostrophe to
occasion: "Time, place, and blood, / How fit you close together!"
(3.3.13-14). Most telling of all, however, is that the Ghost of

Andrugio makes a second appearance and, just when Antonio's vengeance starts to flag, commands again "Revenge!" (3.3.30). For Marston's audience, aware that divine vengeance works in mysterious ways,[10] the pathos inherent in Julio's death is sharply undercut by this supernatural sanction. The blameless Julio's death is a step toward Antonio's revenge in the same way as the blameless Horatio's death is a step toward Andrea's. Antonio says to Julio what Andrea might have said to Horatio: "It is not thee I hate, not thee I kill" (3.3.34).

When next seen, Antonio looks much as Piero did at the start of the play: "his arms bloody, [bearing] a torch and a poniard" (3.5.13.1-2). It has become a critical commonplace that Antonio here visually "becomes his opposite" so that "the moral distinction between Piero and his victims is all but obliterated."[11] Yet the play actually urges a very different interpretation. The physical similarity of Antonio to Piero measures not the distance of Antonio's fall but the degree of his success. The command was "*Scelera non ulcisceris, nisi vincis.*" Lest the audience forget that text, as it might in the shock of Julio's death, the Ghost of Andrugio repeats it, in English, in another charge to his son:

> Fly, dear Antonio.
> Once more assume disguise, and dog the court
> In feignèd habit till Piero's blood
> *May even o'erflow the brim of full revenge.*
> Peace and all blessed fortunes to you both.
> Fly thou from court; *be peerless in revenge.*
> (3.5.24-29; my emphasis)

If vengeance must exceed the injury received, Antonio's bloody entrance is, like the murder of Julio, not the image of his villainy but the measure of his progress along that road of excess leading to the palace of revenge.

That a comparison to Piero is precisely what Antonio seeks, rather than what he unwittingly and villainously reveals, is made quite clear in the next scene. Meditating in his fool's habit upon "a fool's beatitude," Antonio observes,

> Had heaven been kind,
> Creating me an honest, senseless dolt, . . .
> I could not thus run mad

> As one confounded in a maze of mischief
> Staggered, stark felled with bruising stroke of chance;
> I should not shoot mine eyes into the earth,
> Poring for mischief that might counterpoise
> Mischief. . . .
>
> (4.1.48-49, 54-59)

The speech is halted there, with that revelatory statement, by the arrival of Lucio to announce Mellida's trial. The trial brings new mischief: in a trick probably indebted to Lorenzo's method of dispatching Pedringano in *The Spanish Tragedy*, Piero neatly dispenses with Strotzo just after Mellida's honor is finally cleared and Antonio's falsely impugned. For a short while all bodes well for Piero's plans to possess Florence by giving Mellida to Galeatzo and to possess Genoa by making Andrugio's widow his own wife (4.3.136-41). But then, in Piero's first setback, Mellida, thinking Antonio drowned, dies. That death prompts two reactions that together clear the way at last for Antonio's revenge.

Piero's response to Mellida's death is to let his own marriage meats coldly furnish forth his daughter's funeral tables: "I will not stay my marriage for all this!" (4.3.190). In a call to revels strongly reminiscent of Galeatzo's in *Antonio and Mellida*, Piero commands,

> Castilio, Forobosco, all
> Strain all your wits, wind up invention
> Unto his highest bent; to sweet this night,
> Make us drink Lethe by your quaint conceits,
> That for two days oblivion smother grief;
> But when my daughter's exequies approach,
> Let's all turn sighers. Come, despite of fate,
> Sound loudest music; let's pace out in state.
>
> (4.3.191-98)

Thus, in the work of his own hands, does the villain set the occasion.

But revenge's appointed time requires revenge's appointed agent, and Antonio meanwhile has yielded to another slough of Herculean woe. Lost in lyric grief—"O heaven, thou mayst indeed: she was all thine, / All heavenly; I did but humbly beg / To borrow her of thee a little time" (4.4.4-6)—Antonio neglects his vows of vengeance. It is Pandulpho, whose laugh of stoicism has rung as consistently throughout as Piero's laugh of mischief, who reactivates those vows. Casting aside his Senecan pose—"Man will break out, despite philosophy" (4.5.46)—Pandulpho claims for himself the *Ne plus ultra*: "I am the miserablest soul that breathes" (4.5.53). At that challenge to his coveted superlative, Antonio starts up, renews his vow (60), joins Alberto and Pandulpho in digging Feliche's grave with the daggers that will kill Piero, and acknowledges occasion: "Thanks, good old man. We'll cast at royal chance. / Let's think a plot; then pell-mell vengeance!" (4.5.94-95).

The final act begins with the last of the three dumb shows in the play.[12] Since the actions of this show give the crucial final authority to the revenge that is to come, Marston has the Ghost of Andrugio remain on stage to explicate and emphasize:

> The fist of strenuous Vengeance is clutched,
> And stern Vindicta tow'reth up aloft
> That she may fall with a more weighty peise
> And crush life's sap from out Piero's veins.
> Now 'gins the lep'rous cores of ulcered sins
> Wheel to a head; now is his fate grown mellow,
> Instant to fall into the rotten jaws
> Of chapfall'n death. Now down looks providence
> T'attend the last act of my son's revenge.
> Be gracious, Observation, to our scene;
> For now the plot unites his scattered limbs
> Close in contracted bands. The Florence Prince
> (Drawn by firm notice of the Duke's black deeds)
> Is made a partner in conspiracy.
> The States of Venice are so swoll'n in hate
> Against the Duke for his accursèd deeds
> (Of which they are confirm'd by some odd letters
> Found in dead Strotzo's study, which had passed
> Betwixt Piero and the murd'ring slave)
> That they can scarce retain from bursting forth
> In plain revolt. O, now triumphs my ghost,
> Exclaiming, "Heaven's just; for I shall see
> The scourge of murder and impiety."
>
> (5.1.3-25)

Andrugio reaffirms in no uncertain terms the divine sanction ("Now down looks providence") that appoints Antonio's revenge. Equally important, Andrugio emphasizes the human sanction, the sanction of the Senators, the secular authorities, that now approves Antonio's revenge. The central action in the dumb show is this: "Then GALEATZO betwixt two Senators, reading a paper to them; at which they all make semblance of loathing PIERO and knit their fists at him" (5.1.0.4-6). According to Andrugio's explication of the dumb show, that paper is one of "some odd letters / Found in dead Strotzo's study" confirming Piero's deeds. This paper is, then, that second witness mandated by the Mosaic code: "Whosoever killeth anie persone, the judge shal slay the murtherer, through witnesses: but one witnes shal not testifie against a persone to cause him to die" (Numbers 35:30).[13] Only now, after this dumb show, does Antonio's vengeance have the full secular authority it needs.[14] Once that authority is given, there can be little doubt in Marston's audience (and there should be no shock for Marston's modern critics) that the Senators will, in the end, approve Antonio's revenge.

Lest anyone object that this second witness must appear to the revenger himself (as Pedringano's letter does to Hieronimo or Horatio's confirmation of the King's reaction to the Mousetrap does to Hamlet), Marston has the letters cited yet a third time. As the "triumphant revels mount aloft" and "the court is racked to pleasure" (5.3.6, 8), Pandulpho comes running to his fellow masquers. His speech moves precisely as Andrugio's did, from assurance of divine sanction ("Heaven sits clapping of our enterprise" [5.3.15]) to confirmation of Antonio's evidence:

> Now is the plot of mischief ripped wide ope:
> Letters are found 'twixt Strotzo and the Duke
> So clear apparent, yet more firmly strong
> By suiting circumstance, that as I walked
> Muffled, to eavesdrop speech, I might observe
> The graver statesmen whispering fearfully.
>
> (5.3.21-26)

Public approval assured, there remains only the enlistment of Balurdo in the masque (5.3.47-50) before Antonio can at last say to his fellow conspirators Alberto and Pandulpho that the time has come: "Resolved hearts, time curtails night. Opportunity shakes us his foretop. Steel your thoughts, sharp your resolve, embolden your spirit, grasp your swords, alarum mischief . . ." (5.3.59-62).

The masque sequence begins with the entrance of Piero and Maria. As he calls for drink, Piero makes a curious remark that seems to echo Andrugio's wish that Piero's blood would "even o'erflow the brim of full revenge." Piero says, of his goblet, " 'Tis well, brim-full," and then, in a passage that ought, I think, to be marked as an aside, "Even I have glut of blood" (5.4.23). But the glut evidently is not so strong that Piero cannot wish for poison to dispatch a visitor to his victims (5.4.27-29).

The entrance of the four masquers is greeted by Piero's timely query about Julio and Galeatzo's private assurances that the conspirators will be seconded. Piero praises the masquers' "sumptuous pomp" (5.5.10) and calls for the measure, during which the Ghost of Andrugio reappears to sit, like the supernatural solicitors in *The Spanish Tragedy*, "spectator of revenge" (22). With the end of the masque and Piero's call for food, the masque proper seems to be over. But the masquers reject the planned public banquet by asking that the room be cleared until they have eaten. Piero accedes, urging the four—in a line obviously weighted with irony—"Come on, unmask; let's fall to" (31).

But what the conspirators unmask is Piero's mischief, and what they fall to has been called, with some justice, "the most horrible onstage murder in Elizabethan drama."[15] By now, however, it should be clear that the horror is precisely the point; this is indeed "mischief that might counterpoise / Mischief." With Antonio's plucking out of Piero's tongue, Andrugio's Ghost and Heaven are satisfied (36-37). With the tears Piero sheds, Pandulpho is satisfied (44-45; cf. Piero's joy in Antonio's tears at 2.3.125-30). With the presentation of Julio's limbs in "a dish to feast thy father's gorge" (48), each of those who have lost kin—Antonio, Pandulpho, Maria—is satisfied. Even Balurdo has the satisfaction of threatening Piero with the dungeon (37-38). Only when mischief has thoroughly counterpoised mischief is it time to take his life, and even then if vengeance is to exceed injury (*Scelera non ulcisceris, nisi vincis*) it must "let him die and die, and still be dying" (73).

Heaven's ordinance for this vengeance (76-77, 81) is seconded by man's. When Galeatzo and the Senators enter, the three main conspirators (Balurdo is silent) compete for credit. Each thus distinguishes himself from Piero as "a just revenger, a figure who is confident of his cause's righteousness, and who, his vengeance taken, wishes his actions and motives made public."[16] This righteousness is explicitly acknowledged by the magistrates. Here again divine sanction is witnessed (5.6.10-11). Here again civil sanction is given by citation of the letters (14-19). But to these Galeatzo adds the sanction of the ancients: "Thou art another Hercules to us / In ridding huge pollution from our state" (12-13). In vengeance, as in woe, Antonio takes the motto *Ne plus ultra.*

It is fitting, therefore, that Antonio be offered "What satisfaction outward pomp can yield, / Or chiefest fortunes of the Venice state" (23-24). It is also fitting that this Herculean hero out-do Piero once more and choose not pleasure but virtue: "other vows constrain another course" (29).[17]

Modern critics have shown rare unanimity in their distaste for Antonio's revels of revenge. Those concerned with its morality either applaud Marston for condemning it or condemn Marston for applauding it.[18] Those concerned with its dramatic functions and effects dismiss it as token or conventional,[19] or beat it with Hieronimo's stick: "Unlike the fatal masque in *The Spanish Tragedy*, Marston's does not grow out of the structure of the play in any sense, nor does the fatal masque in *Antonio's Revenge* summarize and conclude the thematic action of the work."[20] The few who, like Broude, see in the manner of vengeance something far more complex and dramatically potent than what Arthur Brown called "cramming as much horror and complication as possible into the denouement"[21] have had subjects larger than Marston's play and have given it necessarily cursory attention. Yet there is nothing in the revenge, or in its aftermath, that is not anticipated, accounted for, and—most often—necessitated by some circumstance, some *donnée*, of the play.

Several obstacles prevent students of Marston from seeing the masque in *Antonio's Revenge* as anything more dramaturgically integrated than simply a clever device or theatrical convenience. First, the masque sequence seems short, altogether too brief and too quickly aborted to sustain any rationale for its use. But it is only short on the printed page; it is not short in performance. There is the bustle of the court's entry, an exchange between Piero and Maria that runs for some thirty lines, a song (for which we lack both lyrics and setting), the formal entrance of the masquers, a formal ranking for the measure during which there are two separate conspiratorial exchanges and two brief speeches by Piero, and then the measure itself. There is no reason to suspect that this dance was anything less than a full measure, and it may have been embellished. The length of the English measure varies according to the number of variations it has, but a simple one from a lute book of 1570 is set in fifty-seven measures, and Mabel Dolmetsch required some seven hundred words just to describe the basic steps in the dance.[22] After the measure there is the segment in which the masquers, apparently still masked, persuade Piero to clear the room. Only now can the masque proper fairly be said to be over. Yet the masque seems to continue: the binding and torturing of Piero travesty the traditional gifts given by masquers to the royal spectator. The masque in *Antonio's Revenge* may thus run right up to Galeatzo's entrance, many minutes and some 115 lines after Piero's first entrance.

We can only make informed guesses as to how the Children of Paul's might have distributed themselves about the stage during the masque scene. It would be especially helpful to know a good deal more than we do about the kinds of actions and gestures made by key characters (Antonio, Maria, Pandulpho) during the measure. We do know that "While the measure is dancing, ANDRUGIO'S ghost is placed betwixt the music houses" (5.5.17.1-2); presumably audience attention would be drawn away from the dancers to that spectre. But no one is quite sure what "the music houses" were. Such studies as there are of music in Marston do not help much in ascertaining what kind of song might have been sung before the masque or what kinds of music (other than for the measure) might have been played during the sequence.[23] Certainly the music, the dancing (the measure "was of a serene and graciously undulating character"),[24] and the incantatory language of the scene point toward a stylized and ritualistic effect, but we cannot know precisely how such an effect was achieved in 1601.

Another obstacle faced by many critics is that the masque seems so grotesque as to be parodic.[25] It may well be: taken in isolation, it does seem to glance at atrocities committed by revengers, just and unjust, in such plays as *The Spanish Tragedy* and *Titus Andronicus*. But if the scene is parodic, it is not merely parodic. Taken in context, as the culmination of Antonio's (and Maria's, and Pandulpho's) vengeance against one who has committed less justified and less public atrocities, the masque makes logical, dramaturgical, and even (because the wicked is snared in the work of his own hands) theological sense. The grotesqueness is certainly present, but it responds to Piero's mischiefs and the Ghost's Senecan injunction more directly that it responds to mischiefs in earlier plays.

Finally, there is a tendency to assume that "device" is a pejorative term, that since the masque in *Antonio's Revenge* (or *The Revenger's Tragedy* or *Women Beware Women*) is manifestly a device, it is therefore somehow beneath analysis. The masque in this play *is* a device, but so is the duel in *Hamlet*. That duel is no *deus ex machina*; it is integrated into the play's actions so that it seems an inevitable event. Kyd makes "Soliman and Perseda" seem just as appropriate. Marston's masque is, I have tried to show, equally appropriate, and is thus able to carry with it in performance the burden of all the expectations Marston has been building up in his audience for four acts.

Similar critical reactions have bedeviled Tourneur's *The Revenger's Tragedy*. Yet in Tourneur's play, as in Marston's, the masque of vengeance discharges the debt of injury in precise and particular ways. The particulars, however, do not announce themselves in the masque sequence alone; the actions of the entire play determine both the form and the functions of the masque.

4

Tourneur's *The Revenger's Tragedy*

Of the three masques in Cyril Tourneur's *The Revenger's Tragedy*,[1] the first is reported rather than enacted and the second and third come so close together as to compose one double masque. The first masque, reported by Antonio in the first of his two appearances in the play, was the occasion seized for the rape of Antonio's wife; it has taken place before the action of the play begins. The double masque at the end of the play is made up of two groups of four masquers: the revengers Vindice, Hippolito, and two lords, and the "intended murderers" Ambitioso, Supervacuo, Spurio, and an unnamed fourth. These masques, the one occurring shortly before the start of the play's action and described shortly thereafter and the others occurring together in the final scene, constitute a frame for the play. The skillfully sustained resonances linking these masques are woven throughout the play in such a way that they order its principal action. This action is the action of law, in the form of Vindice's revenges, upon the lust of the ducal court.

The masques in this play have received little critical attention. The first is generally ignored except insofar as it is essential to the plot, while the double masque of revenge is either glossed as mere convention or offered as evidence of Vindice's villainy. The critical tradition in which such commentary stands is derived in large part

45

from the influential study of revenge tragedy written by Fredson Bowers.[2] In tracing this tradition from Bowers to the present, we discover most of the assumptions that underlie interpretations of the masques' functions, in plays like Marston's as well as in Tourneur's.

Although Bowers takes some care to emphasize the ways in which Vindice engages sympathy at the beginning of *The Revenger's Tragedy*, his conclusion is that the hero is exposed at last as villain. Bowers fixes the moment of this exposure at the entrance of Antonio near the end of the play: "the moment Antonio speaks, the spectators are oriented and the true horror of the smirking admissions of Vindice and his brother is realized."[3] This assumption that Antonio is the moral touchstone in the play provides Bowers not only with a rationale for condemning Vindice, but also with a ready explanation for what he calls "the curious moral atrophy of the play."[4] Since Antonio appears only twice in the play—and both times briefly—*The Revenger's Tragedy* all but lacks "the cold reason of a normal person with whom the audience can identify itself."[5] In contrast to Antonio's rationality stands the fatal double masque. Of this Bowers says only that "the revengers achieve their purpose in slaying Lussurioso but there is no indication that the destruction of Spurio and the other brothers is anything more than an unexpected accident in the general tussle."[6] It is difficult to see why the brothers' deaths should be unexpected when they come as a result of the claims and counterclaims to the dukedom which those very brothers have made repeatedly before.[7] This passing reference to the double masque as "the general tussle" exemplifies the thesis Bowers is urging: that the play as a whole suffers from moral atrophy (e.g., the "unexpected accident") stemming in part from the excessive villainy of Vindice (e.g., his unjustified slaying of Lussurioso) and in part from the lack of a touchstone until Antonio enters at the play's end.

The line of interpretation begun by Bowers continues, with some modifications, in Catherine Shaw's discussion of the use of masque in *The Revenger's Tragedy*.[8] Much of what Bowers included under the rubric "curious moral atrophy" is explained by Shaw to be a consequence of the play's genre, which she says is not tragedy but melodrama. Melodrama "has as its purpose the exposure of villainy, vicious licentiousness, and ruthless ambition. It deals in tragic mockery and tragic exaggeration. The audience reaction is one of appalled horror and revulsion."[9] Shaw considers the masques in the light of this generic definition, so that Antonio's report of the early masque is seen to stand in contrast to the violence of the double masque. Antonio's speech "directly links the masque with death and intrigue and . . . is much enhanced by the contrast of its quiet dignity to the vehemence of other speech in the Act."[10] In juxtaposition to this "quiet dignity," Shaw places the final double masque, the key to which she locates in Supervacuo's couplet "A masque is treason's licence, that build upon; / 'Tis murder's best face when a vizard's on."[11] But Supervacuo is patently one of the villains of the piece; it is dangerous to take his definition of a masque as representing either Vindice's view or Tourneur's. Shaw's comments on the masque, however, suggest that she has done precisely that. She stresses the ironies of the sequence: "first Vindici's [*sic*] involved scheme was unnecessary—the murder of Lussurioso would have been committed by the real masquers. Second, Vindici, who has believed his actions justified by divine sanction, attempts to become the moral purger of the whole corrupt court and in so doing becomes as completely evil as the others."[12] Shaw's conclusion is much like Bowers': Vindice is exposed at the end as a ruthless bloodletter, and Antonio alone saves both play and hero from utter degeneration. With Antonio's sentence of execution upon Vindice and Hippolito, Shaw concludes, "the actions upon the stage can then be judged in terms of a moral vision based upon a belief in divine retribution and in the futility of human revenge."[13]

Both Bowers and Shaw interpret the double masque in the light of their views of the play as, respectively, atrophied and melodramatic. They then cite the masques in support of those views. A quite different approach yielding the same conclusion is used by Golding, who begins, as we have seen, with a negative view not of this particular play and its major character but of inserted masques in general and the characters who produce them. Golding wastes no time in declaring his allegiance to Bowers.[14] He quotes Supervacuo's couplet on the masque, explaining that "since this is the nature of Ambitioso's masque, Vindice's identical masque—and Vindice insists upon its being absolutely identical—necessarily takes on the same 'treason's licence' as an essential part of its identity. Thus he becomes as much a murderer through his own perverted taste for devices as all his opponents in the play."[15] But the treason belongs to the ducal brothers alone; Vindice is ambitious not for a dukedom but for revenge. Moreover, Vindice could not possibly insist upon his masque being absolutely identical, since he does not know that the other masquers intend murder.

Several decades ago there was heard a wry complaint that "Tourneur's plays have too often been described as if they were texts for illustration by an Aubrey Beardsley";[16] this is still too often the case, particularly when the descriptions are of the inserted masques. Yet it is possible, I think, to define the place of the inserted masques not in the thesis of the critic but in the dramatic action of the play.

Action in *The Revenger's Tragedy* is ordered by a series of revenges—or attempted revenges—each of which is predicated by a crime of lust. The act of lust need not be sexual; it may also be, as in the case of the ducal brothers' ambition, lust for power. This pattern of lust and law is iterative in the play; it orders the action, rings changes upon repeated emblems and metaphors, and it also couples the masques.

Tourneur's pattern was not a new one. The relationship between lust and law was a frequent topic of proverbs,[17] most of which stressed political implications. The tyrant substituted lust for law in his rule as well as in his means of obtaining power. The good magistrate replaced lust with law. Concise and sententious summaries of this notion are particularly resounding in *Gorboduc*, that dramatic mirror for Queen Elizabeth written by Norton and Sackville early in her reign. Hermon, one of the play's parasitic prompters to evil, reminds Ferrex: "know ye that lust of kingdoms hath no law."[18] The play's most protracted expression of this theme comes as a choral warning:

> When growing pride doth fill the swelling breast
>   And greedy lust doth raise the climbing mind,
> O, hardly may the peril be repressed.
>   Ne fear of angry gods, ne lawes kind,
> Ne country's care can fired hearts restrain
> When force hath armed envy and disdain.
>
> (2.2.89-94)

Here the context is patently political, but "greedy lust" carries its primary sense as well. The warning of dire consequences for replacing law with lust proved to be a common theme not only in Tudor classical tragedy but throughout the drama of the English Renaissance.

Tourneur's achievement is a variation on this theme, a variation consisting primarily in the dramaturgical merging of lust and law into single elements of the play—into an image, a metaphor, an emblem, a repeated scenic design, and a device such as the masque—then untangling the two in ways which give order to the relationship and, through the relationship, the play. The masques represent key sequences in this dramatic organization, but they are by no means the only evidence of its presence. One of the most concise and yet most suggestive of these ambiguous elements is Vindice's use of bone-setting metaphors. Since this metaphor occurs in specific contexts at four different points in the play, it would be illustrative and useful to study those appearances.

In the opening soliloquy, a man holding a skull watches four persons passing in train over the torch-lit stage. Of one of these four "excellent characters" he says (with diction like Hamlet's):

> O, that marrowless age
> Would stuff the hollow bones with damn'd desires,
> And 'stead of heat, kindle infernal fires
> Within the spendthrift veins of a dry duke,
> A parch'd and juiceless luxur.
>
> (1.1.5-9)

The Duke's bones are termed hollow because they lack marrow, but they are actually filled with desires analogous to the fires of luxury running in his veins. What should be aged marrow, the stuff of the Duke's bones, is damned.

The terms of the vehicle in this first speech deserve some emphasis, for the same vehicle is used again in a different but related context. In the interim, however, there is an intriguing exchange between Vindice, in the guise of Piato, and Lussurioso. In the course of the interview, this dialogue occurs:

> Luss. What hast been, of what profession?
> Vind. A bone-setter.
> Luss. A bone-setter?
> Vind. A bawd, my lord; one that sets bones together.
>
> (1.3.42-45)

The lines are too fast-paced, witty, and brutally blunt to be given much allusionistic weight, but they would probably activate in Tourneur's audience two very different associations. One is that suggested by Vindice: the metaphor of bone-setting is a circumlocution for the trade of pander. The other, not present in the lines but called forth by the image of set bones and by the audience's knowledge of Vindice's identity and plots, is more osteopathic. The most famous instance of this sense, an instance quite possibly familiar to many of Tourneur's spectators, is Hamlet's couplet: "The time is out of joint. O cursed spite / That ever I was born to set it right" (*Ham.*, 1.5.188-89). Here the image of personified time in need of bone-setting is very different from the setting of bones performed by bawds. The lines in *Hamlet*, which come just after Hamlet's meeting with the ghost, carry a reference to the commanded revenge that alone can set the time right. In Vindice's lines, the same kind of association between bone-setting and revenge is present, though more subtly.

This association is activated twice again, once in connection with the Duke and once in connection with Lussurioso. Just after the Duke has kissed the poisoned skull of Vindice's betrothed, Vindice exults, "The very ragged bone / Has been sufficiently revenged" (3.5.154-55). This is a crucial statement marking a turning point in the progress of the play as well as in this scene. At this moment, Gloriana's death is declared to have been avenged; "the very ragged bone" is, clearly, the attired skull anointed with poison. Vindice's earlier line about bone-setting as pandering is here visually linked to an act of vengeance. Yet another association of this sort appears in the play's final scene, although this last instance is tied most closely to the first. After the fatal double masque, Antonio pronounces a sentence of death upon the man he finds responsible for the slaughter. "Let him," Antonio orders, "have bitter execution" (5.3.73). With this, Vindice's escape is assured (though only temporarily). His aside makes clear his reaction: "New marrow! No, I cannot be express'd" (5.3.74). This is the marrow of his final revenge,[19] and although this marrow is like that of the "very ragged bone" used in the poisoning scene, the word recalls more immediately the marrow invoked in Vindice's opening soliloquy.

These images of bones and marrow appear at key moments in the play: in the first speech, in the scene where Vindice first adopts his disguise as Piato, in the moment of revenge for Gloriana's death, and in the closing moments. This placement at moments of high dramatic tension within a scene assures emphasis, and emphasis in turn increases the possibility that members of Tourneur's audience would note points of affinity in each context. The effect of the connections serves to lay stress upon the nearly identical nature of lustful action and vengeance. It is a tiny pattern in the mosaic of the play, but it crystallizes an ordering principle operating throughout the whole.

The dramatic portrayal of the various components of this relationship between lust and revenge is nowhere more sharply etched than in the masque sequences. These scenes have much the same allusiveness as the metaphors of bone-setting and bone marrow, but because they are full scenic devices rather than single images they form richer and more ambiguous explorations of the play's central action.

The scene in which the masque of rape is described comes at the end of the first act, which is rather late for an expository inset[20] speech so germane to the plot. Although the Duchess' youngest son is on trial for the rape of Antonio's wife in the second scene, it is not until this fourth scene that the audience learns the circumstances of the crime. This delay in supplying key information allows the audience to focus on, and to establish sympathy for, Vindice's cause for revenge; it also contributes to a sense of accumulating revenges, of a plethora of crimes in a court where men bide their time waiting for an opportunity for vengeance. The trial of the youngest brother in the ducal family has established the fact of the rape (earlier mentioned as "whisper'd" in the court [1.1.109-10]). Antonio's wife is referred to in the present tense, as if alive, throughout the trial scene. With Antonio's report on the rape, the audience learns for the first time not just that it took place under cover of masquery, but also that the victim has died.

The inset masque sequence is also Antonio's first appearance in the play. A stage direction gives his demeanor as "discontented" and indicates that he "discovers" the body of his wife to Piero, Hippolito, and other lords (1.4.0.1-3). Vindice's absence during this scene is significant; it gives the story of the rape a distinctness akin to that of a subplot. Antonio's complaint is parallel to but separate from Vindice's, at least at the start of the play. The sense of a corrupt court in which more than one man has cause for vengeance is underscored by the separation of Antonio from Vindice.

That the lady is dead when she is "discovered" to Antonio's companions is clear from Antonio's description of her as "a fair, comely building newly fall'n" (1.4.2) who, like Lucrece, could not live with such a blot: "Her honour first drunk poison, and her life, / Being fellows in one house, did pledge her honour" (1.4.10-11). The reference to poisoned honor would, of course, invite comparison with the means of Gloriana's death. The effect again is to generalize and broaden the evidence of lustful excess pervading the court.

Antonio's speech comes in response to a request from Hippolito that others be permitted to share the wronged man's grief. It is a detailed and lengthy report:

> Last revelling night,
> When torchlight made an artificial noon
> About the court, some courtiers in the masque,
> Putting on better faces than their own,
> Being full of fraud and flattery—amongst whom,
> The duchess' youngest son (that moth to honour)
> Fill'd up a room; and with long lust to eat
> Into my wearing, amongst all the ladies,
> Singled out that dear form, who ever liv'd
> As cold in lust as she is now in death
> (Which that step-duchess' monster knew too well);
> And therefore, in the height of all the revels,
> When music was heard loudest, courtiers busiest,
> And ladies great with laughter—O, vicious minute,
> Unfit but for relation to be spoke of!—
> Then, with a face more impudent than his vizard,
> He harried her amidst a throng of panders
> That live upon damnation of both kinds,
> And fed the ravenous vulture of his lust
> (O death to think on 't!). She, her honour forc'd,
> Deem'd it a nobler dowry for her name
> To die with poison than to live with shame.
>
> (1.4.26-47)

The tone of this speech has been variously interpreted. Shaw, as noted before, makes much of what she sees as "the contrast of its quiet dignity to the vehemence of other speech in the Act." But another critic labels Antonio's report "a lengthy, graphic, emotional, titillating description of the rape of his wife that contrasts sharply with the stoicism of his earlier exchange with Hippolito."[21] Both of these interpretations are plausible: this is indeed a quieter speech than most of those in previous scenes, yet it also undercuts, as if designed to disprove, Hippolito's misquoted Senecan tag "*Curae leves loquuntur, maiores stupent*" (1.4.23).[22] But the only trustworthy gauge of the speech's tone is the response of Antonio's on-stage audience. Hippolito's reaction is one of admiration for the lady, while Piero's reaction is to demand "what judgment follows the offender?" (1.4.50). Both are engaged sufficiently to take oaths of vengeance upon their swords, and Antonio's mood is clear from his response: "Kind gentlemen, I thank you in mine ire" (1.4.65).

The features of the masque as described by Antonio are torchlight's "artificial noon" (27), the wearing of vizards (29, 41), loud music (38), lust (32, 35, 44), the "vicious minute" of the rape itself (39), and the lady who has drunk poison (45-47). These elements are picked up again at key moments in the play; they are the constituent parts of a carefully constructed accumulation of repeated matter. This repetition joins the action of the masques with the action in certain other key scenes, particularly that in the lodge, and ultimately composes the stuff of the entire play's dramatic fabric.

Illumination of action by torchlight is pervasive in *The Revenger's Tragedy*. It is an atmospheric condition lending tension to moments of high dramatic effect. The very first scene is lit with torchlight (1.1.0.3), and a bit later Vindice cites torches as one of the pleasures of the ducal palace:

> Secured ease and state; the stirring meats,
> Ready to move out of the dishes, that
> E'en now quicken when they're eaten;
> Banquets abroad by torch-light, music, sports,
>
> (2.1.200-03)

Torchlight's power to make night into day is most pronounced in making midnight into noon: Spurio's question when he finds Lussurioso, sword drawn, in the Duke's bedroom is "Ha? what news here? is the day out o' th' socket / That it is noon at midnight?" (2.3.44-45). Midnight is the conventional hour for deeds of darkness. Vindice's assertion that

> Well, if anything

> Be damn'd, it will be twelve o'clock at night,
> That twelve will never 'scape;
> It is the Judas of the hours, wherein
> Honest salvation is betray'd to sin.
>
> (1.3.66-70)

paints every bit as effective a picture as Hamlet's comparable lines:

> 'Tis now the very witching time of night,
> When churchyards yawn, and hell itself breathes out
> Contagion to this world.
>
> (*Ham.*, 3.2.373-75)

or Antonio's in Marston's *Antonio's Revenge*:

> The black jades of swart night trot foggy rings
> 'Bout heaven's brow.
>
> (3.1.1-2)

The other aspect of this inversion is the midnight at noon associated primarily with clandestine and excessive sexual activity. The last line spoken by King Lear's fool, "And I'll go to bed at noon" (*Lr.*, 3.6.83), carries a sexual innuendo in addition to its generalized expression of cosmic disorder. Indulging in sexual pleasures at noon rather than at night carries connotations of lustful, unchaste, and insatiable excess. The place to which Vindice lures the Duke is described as "this unsunned lodge, / Wherein 'tis night at noon" (3.5.18-19; cf. *Women Beware Women*, 4.2.1-10). Both of these inversions of the natural divisions between day and night—torch-light's artificial noon and noon's unsunned and artificial night—are settings in the play for unnatural acts of passion. The unsunned lodge becomes the setting for Vindice's revenge upon the Duke, interrupting the Duke's intended act of lust and substituting the law of vengeance. The only respite from the relentlessly illuminated court comes as a prelude to the banquet and masque prepared for Lussurioso's installation as the new Duke. After the table is brought out, as the new Duke and his followers enter, a blazing star appears. This is a traditional omen of danger, and the fact that it is not noticed for some minutes by those at the banquet renders it more ominous yet. It is, like the thunder that will sound when Lussurioso is stabbed by Vindice, an outward and visible manifestation of heaven's ordinance. Artificial noon and unsunned day are alike eradicated by this

"wondrous dreadful" and "ill-knotted" (5.3.17, 18) harbinger of the
divinely approved human vengeance that waits in the wings.

The wearing of vizards is another element of masquery not
confined to the play's masque scenes. Hippolito calls the skull of
Vindice's betrothed "death's vizard" (1.1.50). Vindice's first interview with Lussurioso includes a discussion of lust during which
Vindice notes how

> Any kin now, next to the rim o' th' sister,
> Is man's meat in these days; and in the morning,
> When they are up and dress'd, and their mask on,
> Who can perceive this?—save that eternal eye,
> That sees through flesh and all.
>
> (1.3.62-66)

The cosmetic function here referred to in terms of a lady's mask is
crucial to Vindice's success in poisoning the Duke. As the two
brothers await the arrival of the party from court, Vindice addresses
the skull of Gloriana: "I'll save your hand that labour; I'll unmask
you" (3.5.48). When the Duke approaches, Vindice chides it, "Hide
thy face now, for shame, thou hadst need have a mask now"
(3.5.114). When Gratiana repents her attempt to barter with her
daughter's honor, Vindice's response indicates that masks serve as
well to protect virtue as to conceal vice: "All mothers that had any
graceful hue / Would have worn masks to hide their face at you"
(4.4.64-65). But the play's most concise comment on vizards is
Supervacuo's definition of a masque: "A masque is treason's licence,
that build upon; / 'Tis murder's best face when a vizard's on"
(5.1.181-82). This quotable couplet is a tempting bait for critics, but
the speaker's identity here colors the words spoken. A masque is
treason's license for Supervacuo, and lust's license for Supervacuo's
younger brother, but it is not necessarily either for Vindice. Insofar
as a masque is revenge's license for Vindice, a vizard serves the same
ends for him as for his enemies. A vizard masks Vindice's law just as
well as it masks the ducal brother's lust.

With the vizards and torchlight of masques comes music, serving similar functions. Antonio's wife is raped "when music was heard
loudest" in the masque. The usefulness of music as a cover for
unpleasant noise had long been exploited by creators of court entertainments and pageantry for royal progresses. Although *The*

Masque of Queens, with its major scene change after the (then still new) antimasque, had not yet been performed when Tourneur wrote his play, music's ability to conceal other noise would be obvious to any audience. When Vindice includes music among the attractions which the ducal palace would hold for Castiza and Gratiana (2.1.203, quoted above), Tourneur's audience might have heard ominous overtones. Music's main part in the tragedy is played as the Duke lies dying in the unsunned lodge. First, the approach of the Duchess and Spurio is heralded by music (3.5.189, 206). Then, as the Duke is forced to look on, the Duchess invites Spurio in to their appointed rendezvous: "let's in, and feast. / Loud'st music sound; pleasure is banquet's guest" (3.5.220-21). Vindice and his brother later pay tribute to the way music muffled their loud revenge:

> Vind.   The brook is turn'd to blood.
> Hipp.   Thanks to loud music.
> Vind.   'Twas our friend indeed.
> 'Tis state in music for a duke to bleed.
>   (3.5.222-24)

Music also serves figurative ends at several points in the play. When Vindice enters just as Lussurioso is recounting his treachery to Hippolito, Hippolito calls attention to the danger in an aside: "'Sfoot, just upon the stroke / Jars in my brother; 'twill be villainous music" (4.1.26-27). Near the end of the play, Vindice encourages his followers with these words: "My lords, be all of music; strike old griefs / Into other countries" (5.2.1-2). Music accompanies the dumb show of Lussurioso's installation as Duke (5.3.0.2). But in an omen comparable to the blazing star's appearance, the music of Vindice's final act of revenge comes from heaven. In response to the invocation to "almighty patience"—"Is there no thunder left" (4.2.198)—the first clap is heard. And at the moment when the first group of masquers becomes the manifestation of the blazing star's omen, the "big-voic'd cryer" (5.3.42) is heard again.

The importance of poisoning in The Revenger's Tragedy has often been noted by critics. But the particular way in which the use of poison links the reported masque of rape with Vindice's revenge has received little critical attention. The play's many poisonings underscore the ways in which the act of revenge is designed by the revenger to imitate the crime. Since Vindice's skull is a "sallow picture of my poison'd love" (1.1.14), it determines the manner of revenge:

> I have not fashion'd this only for show
> And useless property; no, it shall bear a part
> E'en in it own revenge. This very skull,
> Whose mistress the duke poison'd, with this drug,
> The mortal curse of the earth, shall be reveng'd
> In the like strain, and kiss his lips to death.
>
> (3.5.100-05)

Hippolito's response to this is significant: he applauds the constancy of his brother's vengeance and the "quaintness" of his brother's malice (3.5.108-09; cf. 4.2.5). What Hippolito terms the "quaintness" of Vindice's revenge is precisely its cleverness, the way in which Vindice has suited the act of revenge to the act of poisoning by making the revenge itself a poisoning. Since the audience watches as Gloriana's own skull causes the Duke's lingering death, there is an unmistakable image of Gloriana avenging her own death. The fact that Antonio's wife is also dead from poison links the vengeance of Antonio with the vengeance of Vindice. Yet the offender in the latter case, the Duchess' youngest son, meets his own end not through a contrived act of revenge but through accident, through a chance mistaking of the identity of a condemned man.

Both these kinds of retribution—the one controlled by human design and craft, the other under the aegis of chance and fate—take place within a dramatically ordered frame of time. The characters' repeated deplorings of lust's "vicious minute" and their recurrent invocations of opportunity are illustrative of a connection between the progress of time in the play and the movement from lust to law.

We have heard Kyd's Hieronimo and Marston's Antonio invoke the notion that revenge has a particular moment. In Tourneur's play, the character who most frequently voices this is, naturally, Vindice. In the first scene, he apostrophizes,

> Vengeance, thou murder's quit-rent, and whereby
> Thou show'st thyself tenant to Tragedy,
> O, keep thy day, hour, minute, I beseech,
> For those thou hast determin'd!
>
> (1.1.39-42)[23]

The moment of Vindice's vengeance is the moment of the old Duke's death, as the rhetorical stress on the word "minute" indicates: "Now nine years' vengeance crowd into a minute!" (3.5.123).[24]

But these intermediate acts of vengeance are at the last subsumed by those in the final scene of masquery. In this scene, the strands which we have seen carried through the play are woven into a spectacular and bloody staging of multiple revenges.

The scene begins with a striking series of tableaux: the dumb show of Lussurioso's possessing,[25] the bringing on of the banquet table, and the appearance of a blazing star. The star's ominous effect is reinforced by Lussurioso's announcement, in an aside, that he intends to purge what remains of his family (5.3.7-11), and also by the ease with which the new Duke accepts the flattery of his fawning noblemen. He accords the place of honor at his side to that noble who wishes him immortality, then sits down to watch the masque.

The masque of revengers enters first. It is clear from Lussurioso's recognition of them as "Brothers, and bastard" (5.3.41) that Vindice and his followers have successfully upstaged the intended masquers. Tourneur's audience had been informed of the plan previously, when Vindice explained it to his companions:

> You shall have all enough;—revels are toward,
> And those few nobles that have long suppress'd you
> Are busy'd to the furnishing of a masque,
> And do affect to make a pleasant tale on 't;
> The masquing suits are fashioning; now comes in
> That which must glad us all—we to take pattern
> Of all those suits, the colour, trimming, fashion,
> E'en to an undistinguish'd hair almost;
> Then, ent'ring first, observing the true form,
> Within a strain or two we shall find leisure
> To steal our swords out handsomely,
> And when they think their pleasure sweet and good,
> In midst of all their joys, they shall sigh blood.
>
> (5.2.10-22)

Execution of the plan proceeds without flaw, leaving the new Duke and his fawning noblemen dead in their chairs. Thunder is heard for the second time in the play in acknowledgment of Vindice's deeds. He, in turn, acknowledges the sound: "No power is angry when the lustful die; / When thunder claps, heaven likes the tragedy" (5.3.46-47). As Vindice moves off the stage, the masque of intended murderers—Ambitioso, Supervacuo, Spurio, and the unlucky fourth—comes on. But before their measure is done, Lussurioso's groans halt them in their dance, and the murders are discovered. There follows a group of stabbings[26] that leaves all three brothers dead and the fourth nobleman alone standing to answer for the slaughter.

In the small space of some ten lines, both sets of masquers have entered, danced, and ended their revels in blood. Yet in the time between the first group's entrance and the arrival of Antonio, there are seven deaths. Since every member of the ducal family is killed, the revenge of Vindice, Hippolito, and their followers seems complete. Antonio, too, has had his wrongs requited. "The rape of your good lady has been quited / With death on death," Vindice observes. And Antonio gives assent: "Just is the law above!" (5.3.90-91).

But just at this moment, when Vindice and Antonio have together given voice to the justice of the law which quits the debt owed by lust, when the masque of revenge has paid the charge incurred by the masque of rape, Antonio ventures to inquire how the old Duke was murdered. In a stunningly swift reversal of their fortunes, Vindice and Hippolito are seized and ordered off to "speedy execution" while Antonio justifies their deaths: "Away with 'em! Such an old man as he; / You that would murder him would murder me" (5.3.104-05).

This remarkable and unexpected final event is generally glossed as Vindice's just reward in Antonio's finest hour—vice punished and virtue duly rewarded. The text, however, supports another reading. Antonio's reasoning is spurious at best; their revenge completed, Vindice and Hippolito lack cause to murder Antonio. Vindice calls Antonio's attention to this fact: "Thou hast no conscience; are we not reveng'd? / Is there one enemy left alive amongst those?" (5.3.108-09). Nor does either brother seek the dukedom, for they recognize in Antonio "the hope / Of Italy" and "the silver age again" (5.3.84-86). Their claim of credit for the Duke's murder is not the act of villainous fools; it is evidence that Vindice and Hippolito, like Hieronimo and Marston's Antonio, are revengers confident of their cause's justice, proud of their revenge's "quaintness," and sure

in their public defense: "All for your grace's good. We may be bold
to speak it now; 'twas somewhat wittily carried, though we say it"
(5.3.96-97). It is less Vindice's confession than Antonio's reaction to
the confession that is surprising. Antonio is not Marston's Galeatzo
proclaiming the revenging hero "another Hercules"; he is more like
the King of Spain proclaiming Hieronimo a "traitor." Vindice's last
speech is only partially the self-laceration of an "ass" (5.1.158) who
finds himself in a newly cleansed court. The speech also vents the
bitterness of heaven's scourge confronted with a mortal blindness
that punishes the just revenger as severely as a villain. Finally, like
Hieronimo, Vindice can only accept a death softened by the consola-
tion of success:

> This work was ours, which else might have been slipp'd,
> And, if we list, we could have nobles clipp'd,
> And go for less than beggars; but we hate
> To bleed so cowardly. We have enough, i'faith;
> We're well, our mother turn'd, our sister true;
> We die after a nest of dukes. Adieu.
>
> (5.3.120-25)[27]

The problems that plague analysis of Marston's revels of revenge persist in Tourneur's. The masque sequence that seems so
short and inadequate in the text requires some minutes, and some
complexity of movement, in performance. It includes a masquers'
entry, a dance, four murders, a second entry of new masquers, and a
second dance (this one specifically called a "measure" at 5.3.48.5).
Here again the skeletal stage directions do no more than hint at how
the scene might have been staged in the first decade of the seventeenth century. It must have been one of high dramatic tension and
strong theatrical effectiveness, if only because it brings virtually the
entire cast onto the stage in an orgy of death and revelation. Any one
of a number of other such devices might have served Tourneur for
his climactic scene, but none so well, given the events of the play
thus far, as this double masque. The many associations that masques
and masquers, visors and music, torchlight and revels have acquired
in the previous four and a half acts all cling to this double dance of
masquing murderers and give it a rich resonance that is not evident
in the isolated scene. In the text as we have it, the masque seems

pitifully unelaborated, too briefly sketched to carry all those associations thrust upon it by earlier words and deeds. But this cannot be the case in performance, where any dance, any gesture, any torchlight, any visor worn or music heard is an elaboration, a way of filling in the sketch.

5

Beaumont and Fletcher's
The Maid's Tragedy

The nuptial entertainment in Beaumont and Fletcher's *The Maid's Tragedy* is a spectacular anomaly among masques in Renaissance tragedy. It occurs not in the fifth act but in the first; it is far longer than most masques within plays, running to some 165 lines (with the additions from the second quarto of 1622) and accounting for over a third of the first act; it is performed not by characters from the *dramatis personae* of the play proper but by masquers who do not appear again in the action; it is uninterrupted, running its full course from the entry of Night through three songs and three measures to its appointed close; it lacks revels and so interacts with its on-stage audience only in its conventional bow to King, bride, and bridegroom; and, most significantly, the masque leaves unresolved an important development that threatens both its own internal logic and the future of the couple it is intended to honor. By the winter playing season of 1610–1611, when *The Maid's Tragedy* was most likely first performed, each of these features presented a notable departure from precedent. Masques of this fullness had been seen a few times in comedy, or in Fletcher's new tragicomedy, but not in tragedy.

The date and venue of this play's first performances are important. On the 31st of October 1611 the Master of the Revels, Sir

George Buc, wrote on a manuscript, "This second Maydens tragedy (for it hath no name inscribed) may with the reformations bee acted publikely."[1] Scholars and editors agree that "Buc's terminology suggests that he had recently licensed *The Maid's Tragedy* itself."[2] The title page of Q1, printed in 1619, the same year the play was entered in the Stationers' Register, notes that "it hath beene divers times Acted at the Black-friers by the King's Majesties Servants."[3] Evidently, then, the play was among those first performed by the King's Men after their move into winter quarters at the Blackfriars; it is one of only "two extant plays probably written for performance at the Blackfriars during the period 1609–13 (*The Maid's Tragedy* and *The Two Noble Kinsmen*)."[4] In addition, *The Maid's Tragedy* was one of the fourteen plays performed by the King's Men at court early in 1613 in honor of Princess Elizabeth's marriage to the Elector Palatine.[5]

Also performed at court that winter was *The Masque of The Inner Temple and Gray's Inn*, written by Francis Beaumont. It was Beaumont, scholars agree, who wrote seven of the eleven scenes in *The Maid's Tragedy*, including both of those in the first act.[6] It was Beaumont, then, who in all probability wrote the masque sequence. Both the masque in the play and the one given at court two years later show that their author kept abreast of Ben Jonson's contributions to the genre. At least two, and perhaps three, of Jonson's masques are especially pertinent to the entertainment in *The Maid's Tragedy: Beauty*, for its portrayal of the winds Boreas and Vulturnus, *Hymenaei*, for its celebration of union and for an incipient rebellion early in its action, and perhaps also *Queens*, for its antimasque.

The textual history of *The Maid's Tragedy*, once very confused and still slightly uncertain, is another extradramatic factor relevant to the inserted masque.[7] The play was clearly quite popular; it had seven quarto editions before appearing in the second Beaumont and Fletcher folio of 1679. These eight editions descend lineally except for F2, which derives from Q6 rather than Q7; only the first three provide authoritative readings. Q3 is the least important of the three because it is, but for some seventy substantive variants, a reprint of Q2. Q2, printed in 1622 from Q1 and claiming on its title page to be "newly perused, augmented, and inlarged," adds about eighty lines and numerous variant readings for both substantives and accidentals. Of Q2's additional lines, some twenty-five belong to the masque: ten lines of Cynthia's second speech (1.2.140−49) and about fifteen lines from the second measure through the third song and third measure (1.2.235−48). Any discussion of the masque, then, must decide first whether these are to be accepted as authorial interpolations and, second, whether the masque was cut or enlarged.

On the first question there is no disagreement; the lines in Q2 that are not in Q1 are universally accepted as authorial. The second point, however, is troublesome because deciding whether the masque was cut or enlarged requires positing a relationship between Q1 and Q2. Until only a decade ago, Q2 was invariably selected as copy-text for editions of *The Maid's Tragedy* on the grounds, apparently corroborated by the title page, that it incorporated authorial additions and revisions. Q1 was then seen as a cut version of whatever papers served as printer's copy for Q2. The cutting was evidently done for performance: "none of the passages removed leaves a serious break in the logic of the action, and the inference from this fact must be that the text was deliberately and thoughtfully cut, one can only suppose with performance in view."[8] But in 1968, Howard Norland published an edition of *The Maid's Tragedy* that used Q1 as copy-text "because it is the anterior text in the ancestral series."[9] Norland adopted all substantive variants from Q2 (except obvious compositorial errors) "since Q2 appears to embody authorial revision of the earlier text."[10] He admits that the ten lines added to Cynthia's speech "may have been included in the foul papers but because of extensive revision were thought by the compositor (or the scribe) to be cancelled."[11] But, Norland says, "the addition of a new song along with introductory dialogue in the masque . . . would seem to indicate a further development or heightening of the dramatic situations made at a later time."[12] Norland does not suggest that this addition is non-authorial, simply that it was made later than the surrounding material; in other words, the masque was enlarged, not cut. Andrew Gurr, introducing his old-spelling edition of 1969, concurs: "it is fairly clear that the copy used for the Q2 annotations was a later version of the play than the Q1 copy."[13]

Many of the conclusions of Norland and Gurr were based on Robert Turner's dissertation and articles,[14] and in 1970 Turner himself did an edition, using Q1 as copy-text, for Fredson Bowers' complete edition of the plays in the Beaumont and Fletcher canon. Turner's thorough consideration of the evidence leads him to these conclusions:

> Ambiguous though it often is, the evidence points toward a history of the text which may be recapitulated as follows: Q1 was printed from late-stage foul papers in Beaumont's hand. . . . Q2 was printed from a copy of Q1 into which had been introduced readings from a fair copy of the foul papers, probably also written out by Beaumont, who made some changes in the process.[15]

This statement, which agrees with Norland's view in the essentials, appears to work against Turner's earlier suggestion of theatrical abridgment. He admits, in fact, that the songs added in the masque and in the following scene (Aspatia's "Lay a garland on my hearse / Of the dismall Yew" and Dula's "I could never have the power") are perhaps significant enough to be seen as "augmentations of an early version."[16] And Turner later writes that "cutting suggests theatrical provenience; however, there are few features of Q1 that connect it with the theater and some features that point away from such a connection."[17] The weight of what little evidence there is would appear to lean toward the likelihood that the masque was authorially enlarged, not cut, at some point in the history of its early performances, and that the conflated version—Q1's text with the Q2 additions—represents the authors' final intentions as to what their audience should have.[18]

The masque in *The Maid's Tragedy* has summoned three rather different kinds of critical responses. A very few have dismissed it as a sop to the Blackfriars and court audiences, an excrescence more or less irrelevant to the action of the play: "il ne se rattache que de très loin à l'action et n'est qu'une petite pièce de circonstance."[19] A much more typical response, however, is to observe the masque's ironic relationship to the ensuing events in the play. Ewbank, for example, cites several ways in which the conventional themes of the nuptial masque are used as foils to the actual wedding night of Evadne and Amintor: "the authors have seized on the assumptions of the traditional marriage masque—pre-nuptial chastity, bridal bliss and royal integrity—and contrasted them with a corrupt reality; and so, albeit in an obvious way, the masque is used dramatically rather than as mere spectacular padding."[20] Catherine Shaw also

sees the masque as ironic, but in her comments the patronizing note
sounded by Ewbank ("albeit in an obvious way") is louder:

> Although, perhaps, its very elaborateness detracts somewhat from its
> effectiveness, the function of this masque is again to provide ironic
> juxtaposition. . . . The actual masque serves of less value to the dra-
> matic unity or progression of the play than we have been led to
> expect. It does, however, enhance the irony of the happy celebration
> of a marriage which was conceived in evil, caused such unhappiness,
> and brought such disaster.[21]

The problem for both Ewbank and Shaw is that the irony is indeed
obvious, so much so that pointing out the ways in which it works
sound to each critic like a necessary but not especially productive
task.

But there is a less obvious feature of the masque to which a
small third school of critics has been attentive. William W. Appleton
was among the first to emphasize that the masque is not merely (and
obviously) ironic in retrospect, from the vantage point of the fifth
act, but also prophetically ironic—from the vantage point of the first
act.[22] Two decades earlier, M. C. Bradbrook had written laconically
that "the masque in *The Maid's Tragedy*, with its description of
'sudden storm' rising on the marriage night, is not entirely irrelevant."[23] Clifford Leech explained that the reported escape of
Boreas is "an ill omen for the marriage that is being celebrated,"[24]
and Suzanne Gossett stressed that Boreas not only escapes but "is
not yet recaptured as the masque ends."[25]

Appleton, Bradbrook, Leech, and Gossett are all arguing that
the masque was ominous and prophetic as well as retrospectively
ironic, that it was an anticipation of the action as well as a foil to it.
Michael Neill goes further: "the whole of the ensuing play action
can be seen as the process by which the ambiguities of the masque
are ironically elaborated and finally resolved."[26] In his long and
convincing article, Neill concentrates on the various ways in which
the masque's equivocal imagery—of night and day, dark and light—
is exploited throughout the play until finally resolved in the closing
scenes. The equivocation, Neill says, fastens itself mainly to the
sexual and literal meanings of the word "die," until

> in its final act *The Maid's Tragedy* is revealed as at once dramatized
> epitaph and epithalamium; the disturbing ambiguities of the masque

have been elaborated into a structure of verbal and dramatic ironies which, whatever the difference of scale, is fundamentally of the same order, in its witty conjunction of opposites, as Herrick's "Upon a maid that dyed the day she was married."[27]

Neill's main interest is clearly in the verbal patterning of the masque and in the imagery and rhetorical equivocations of the play. He devotes comparatively little space, however (two pages of some twenty-four), to the *incident* that, although reported and not enacted, dominates the masque: the escape of Boreas. Neill does call attention to the several points at which this escape reappears in the imagery of later speeches,[28] but he neglects important analogues in the action of subsequent scenes. To the verbal patterns that Neill properly sees as fixing the masque firmly in the play we may, I think, add patterns of dramatic action that contribute no less significantly to what M. C. Bradbrook, again laconically, has called the "felt fusion" of masque and play.[29]

The masque in *The Maid's Tragedy* begins with the entry of Night, who calls immediately for the radiance of Cynthia, goddess of the moon and of chastity. Cynthia delivers the conventional "praise / Of the assembly" earlier promised by Strato (1.1.8-9):

> Great Queen they be a troop for whom alone,
> One of my clearest moones I have put on,
> A troope that lookes as if thy selfe and I,
> Had pluckt our reines in, and our whips laid by
> To gaze upon these mortals, that appeare
> Brighter than we.
>
> (1.2.128-33)

Night suggests that, to honor the occasion, Cynthia call forth nymphs and shepherds or Endymion (150-57), but the goddess denies the story of her love for Endymion (158-61)[30] and determines instead to "give a greater state and glory, / And raise to time a nobler memory / Of what these lovers are" (162-64).

Neptune rises in answer to Cynthia's call and receives this charge:

> Hie thee then,
> And charge the Winde goe from his rockie den,
> Let loose his subjects, onely *Boreas*
> Too foule for our intensions as he was,

> Still keepe him fast chain'd, we must have none here
> But vernall blasts and gentle winds appeare,
> Such as blow flowers, and through the glad bowes sing,
> Many soft welcomes to the lusty spring.
>
> (172-79)

Neptune passes the order to Eolus, god of the winds, commanding him explicitly to "free, / *Favonius* and thy milder winds to waite / Upon our *Cinthia*, but tie *Boreas* straight, / Hee's too rebellious" (187-90). No sooner does Eolus retreat to his rock, though, then he returns to tell Neptune that "*Boreas* has broke his chaine, / And strugling with the rest has got away" (193-94). But Neptune merely sends Eolus back to fetch Proteus and does not seem concerned about Boreas' escape: "Let him alone, ile take him up at sea, / He will not long be thence" (195-96).

The threat posed by Boreas is forgotten in the ensuing three songs and three measures. But as the third of these dances ends, Eolus returns again to Neptune:

> The sea goes hie,
> *Boreas* hath rais'd a storme, goe and apply
> Thy trident, else I prophesie, ere day
> Many a tall ship will be cast away,
> Desend with all the gods and all their powre,
> To strike a calme.
>
> (249-54)

Since Neptune and his companions are now urgently needed, Cynthia thanks all the gods and sends them back in haste "Least your proud charge should swell above the wast, / And win upon the Iland" (261-62).

On that command, Neptune and the gods of the wind and sea descend. Since the approaching dawn very shortly sends Cynthia into day and Night back into mists, the threat posed by Boreas is left unresolved. Whether Boreas will in fact be tamed remains for the play to decide.

In the conceit of the nuptial masque, the taming of Boreas is a task left undone partly because it is the job of the bride and bridegroom to do it. The rebellion of Boreas is first of all a sexual metaphor. Only the wedding night can determine whether the storm will be calmed, or whether the "proud charge should swell above the wast" and "ere day / Many a tall ship will be cast away." The *doubles entendres* are quite evident, and we should not be so solemn about the headier implications of Boreas' escape that we miss the sexual point. On the other hand, the rebellion of the north wind is assuredly more than a sexual joke. For those many members of Beaumont and Fletcher's audience familiar with other masques portraying the north wind and rebellions, there were less lusty and more ominous associations.

Not long before *The Maid's Tragedy* was first performed, Ben Jonson had put Boreas into his *Masque of Beauty*. This masque, which was a sequel to *Blackness*, Jonson's first court masque, had been intended for the 1606 season but was twice postponed when nuptial masques were needed instead. It was finally performed at Whitehall on the Sunday after Twelfth Night of 1608.[31] In his notes to the masque, Jonson explains that, in order to bring news of the *Blackness* masquers from the sea, he

> induced Boreas, one of the winds, as my fittest messenger, presenting him thus: In a robe of russet and white mixed, full and bagged, his hair and beard rough and horrid, his wings grey and full of snow and icicles, his mantle borne from him with wires, and in several puffs, his feet ending in serpents' tails, and in his hand a leafless branch laden with icicles.
>
> (Beauty, 8-13)

Although Boreas does not actually appear in *The Maid's Tragedy*, Jonson's description, which derives from classical sources,[32] is probably a fair summary of the associations the name had for both the Blackfriars and court audiences to the play. In *The Masque of Beauty*, Boreas brings to Januarius a report that the "twelve Ethiop dames" (42) from *Blackness* are now at the mercy of envious Night's "malice and her magic" (70). The bearer of woeful tidings is rewarded with this from Januarius:

> Would thou had'st not begun, unlucky wind,
> That never yet blew'st goodness to mankind,
> But with thy bitter and too piercing breath
> Strik'st horrors through the air as sharp as death.
>
> (92-95)

But just then the sweeter east wind arrives:

> All horrors vanish, and all name of death!
> Be all things here as calm as is my breath.

A gentler wind, Vulturnus, brings you news
The isle is found, and that the nymphs now use
Their rest and joy. The Night's black charms are flown.
                                                    (100-04)

The remainder of Vulturnus' speech is an elaborate presentation of
the sixteen main masquers, and both winds depart very soon after
the discovery of the central scene. In both his habit and the news he
brings, Boreas is the ill wind that blows no man good; Jonson
dispenses with both the wind and the message as neatly as he will
later and more magnificently dispense with the hags in *Queens*.
Boreas and his tale amount to an incipient antimasque in *Beauty*,
and Jonson—unlike Beaumont and Fletcher—wastes no time in
obliterating the threat.

   A different but no less significant antecedent to the masque in
The Maid's Tragedy is provided by Jonson's nuptial masque *Hymenaei*, one of the wedding entertainments that postponed *Beauty*
(the other was Thomas Campion's *Lord Hay's Masque*, performed
in 1607). Here it is not the northern wind's presence but the nuptial
occasion that invites comparison to the masque in *The Maid's Tragedy*. And perhaps this is the place to recall that the retrospective
ironies of art sometimes held true in life: *Hymenaei* honored a
marriage that also ended, unconsummated, in scandal. Cyrus Hoy
sees here a mannerist dislocation: "viewed with the knowledge of
hindsight, masques like *Hymenaei* and *A Challenge at Tilt*—
wherein all the powers of virtuous love are invoked to celebrate the
two marriages of Lady Frances Howard—seem almost too blatant
examples of idealism come unhooked from the occasions it was
intended to inform."[33] The analogy to the situation in *The Maid's
Tragedy* is obvious, though in *Hymenaei* there was no rebellious
Boreas to foreshadow the unhooking.

   There is in *Hymenaei*, however, a rebellion of another sort.
After the first song and Hymen's first speech, "Union's gracious rites
are suddenly disturbed."[34]

   Here out of a microcosm, or globe, figuring man, with a kind of
   contentious music, issued forth the first masque, of eight men. These
   represented the four humors and four affections, all gloriously attired,
   distinguished only by their several ensigns and colors, and dancing out

on the stage, in their return at the end of their dance drew all their
swords, offered to encompass the altar and disturb the ceremonies.
(Hymenaei, 98-103)

At this, Hymen calls for help:

> Save, save the virgins; keep your hallowed lights
> Untouched, and with their flame defend our rites.
> The four untempered humors are *broke out*,
> And with their wild affections go about
> To ravish all religion. If there be
> A power like reason left in that huge body,
> Or little world of man, from whence these came,
> Look forth, and with thy bright and numerous flame
> Instruct their darkness, make them know and see,
> In wronging these, they have *rebelled* 'gainst thee.
> (105-14; my emphasis)

There is indeed, it develops, "a power like reason left" in the
microcosm; it is Reason herself, a lamp in one hand and a bright
sword in the other (119), who now descends and speaks. At her
words, "the humors and affections sheathed their swords and retired
amazed to the sides of the stage, while Hymen began to rank the
persons and order the ceremonies" (140-42). From this point to the
masque's close the four humors and four affections dance not to
"contentious music" but in pairs and in union, ranked with the eight
ladies they now obey, and led by the servant of Reason, Order. At
the end, they "in their latter strain fell into a fair orb or circle,
Reason standing in the midst" (359-60). The rebellion is quelled,
humor and affection are made to obey reason, and the incipient
antimasque is made to serve the masque by joining in its celebration
of nuptial union. The Boreas of *Hymenaei* is tamed.

The crux of the second act of *The Maid's Tragedy* is Amintor's
(and the audience's) discovery that both his bride and his King have
allowed their humors and affections to rebel against reason and the
rites of union. The problem for Amintor, then, is that, as Calianax
says in another context, "The King may doe this, and he may not doe
it" (2.2.81). The major question for the remaining three acts is
whether a king's subject may defy order, break his chain, raise a
storm, and rebel against a king who has rebelled against union. The
answer, as usual in Beaumont and Fletcher, is not simple: "on

lustfull Kings / Unlookt for suddaine deaths from God are sent, / But curst is he that is their instrument" (5.3.293-95).

For Amintor, the very name of King (and in this play the King has no other name) forbids rebellion. Though in his first vengeful anger at Evadne's revelation he had promised retribution ("let me know the man that wrongs me so, / That I may cut his body into motes, / And scatter it before the Northren winde" [2.1.297-99]), her naming of the man instantly stays his hand:

> Oh thou hast nam'd a word that wipes away
> All thoughts revengefull, in that sacred name,
> The King, there lies a terror, what fraile man
> Dares lift his hand against it? let the Gods
> Speake to him when they please, till when let us
> Suffer, and waite.
>
> (2.1.306-11)

Amintor reiterates this conviction for the King himself:

> as you are meere man,
> I dare as easily kill you for this deede,
> As you dare thinke to doe it, but there is
> Divinitie about you, that strikes dead
> My rising passions; as you are my King,
> I fall before you and present my sword,
>
> (3.1.237-42)

So determined is Amintor to suffer and be silent that he draws his sword on his friend Melantius for urging revenge (3.2.180-259). Later, however, rage breaks out despite conviction, and Amintor at last concludes the King must be killed (4.2.289-97). Melantius, who has other plans for the King (because "the wicked is snared in the worke of his owne hands"), attempts an appeal to Amintor's reason: "let your reason / Plot your revenge, and not your passion" (4.2.298-99). But reason, although it worked in *Hymenaei*, will not calm the nominalist Amintor; only Melantius' repeated naming of the King can do that: "I cannot tell / What thou hast said, but thou hast charmd my sword / Out of my hand" (4.2.311-13). The implicit comparison with a Boreas bound is made quite explicit when Amintor reacts to the blood on Evadne's hands: "thou hast toucht a life / The very name of which had power to *chaine* / *Up* all my rage, and *calme* my wildest wrongs" (5.3.136-38; my emphasis).

Since Amintor rejects the analogue of rebellion in the masque, it is left to Melantius and Evadne to break the great chain of being and rebel against their sovereign. Melantius had allied himself from the very start with the kind of contentious music that accompanied Jonson's humors and affections: "These soft and silken warres are not for me, / The musicke must be shrill and all confus'd / That stirs my blood, and then I daunce with armes" (1.1.41–43). Though he is slow to believe Amintor's report that Evadne is the King's whore, Melantius once convinced does not hesitate to vow revenge (3.2.190–95, 201–02, 213). The honor of friend and of family is greater to him than the name of King (3.2.245–48). In persuading Evadne that revenge is her responsibility, Melantius buttresses the rationale he gave Amintor with the sanction of divine mandate: "No al the gods require it, / They are dishonored in him" (4.1.145–46).

The central act of rebellion in *The Maid's Tragedy* is the regicide, and the anticipatory significance of Boreas' escape inheres in that act. In Jonson's *Masque of Beauty* the ill wind brought by Boreas had been expunged by a gentler wind announcing the safe arrival of majesty. In *Hymenaei* the sedition, analogous to the northern wind's rebellion, is dispelled not merely by order and reason in the microcosm and in the union of marriage but also, as D. J. Gordon has so carefully shown, by harmony in the union of a kingdom under the sway of a virtuous sovereign. The rebellion of Boreas in the masque in *The Maid's Tragedy* anticipates not merely an absence of union in the marriage, but also an absence of union in the kingdom. That union is only supplied when the King is replaced. There is far more than a leer in Cynthia's command to Neptune: "Now back unto your government in hast, / Least your proud charge should swell above the wast, / And win upon the Iland."

To submit that the masque in *The Maid's Tragedy* is anticipatory is not at all to deny that it is also, as many critics have observed, an ironic foil. On the contrary, the dramatic power of the masque in its complex relationship to the play resides in the ways it is *both* foil and foresight. Imbuing a dramatic event with this kind of double aspect ("The King may doe this, and he may not doe it") is characteristic of Beaumont and Fletcher. The closest analogy in *The Maid's Tragedy* is the double play on the name "Evadne": its association with that virtuous Greek lady who killed herself on her husband's funeral pyre so that she might be with him even in death is both an

ironic foil to Evadne's conduct on her wedding night and an anticipation of her suicide in front of the husband she has come to love.
Ultimately there is the double aspect of the regicide itself, which
carries both heaven's sanction and the new King's curse: "on lustfull
Kings / Unlookt for suddaine deaths from God are sent, / But curst is
he that is their instrument." That "but" forbids a neat resolution.
The audience to *The Maid's Tragedy* is left with a promise that
Melantius will follow Amintor in death (5.3.288-90). It is a promise
that strangely echoes Neptune's "ile take him up at sea, / He will not
long be thence."

6

Webster's *The Duchess of Malfi*

The anomalous features of the masque in *The Maid's Trag-edy*—its length and fullness, its appearance very early in the play, its lack of revels—serve to concentrate the spectator's attention on the masque itself, rather than on the character who produces it or on the reactions of an on-stage audience. Although Calianax is clearly responsible for certain aspects of the masque's production, the text gives no reason to suppose that he wrote it or designed it or that it serves any purpose of his as, for example, Hamlet's "Mousetrap" serves him. In fact, Calianax has rather strong objections to his task (1.2.16-19). None of the characters in *The Maid's Tragedy* ever comments on the masque, which ends abruptly and without the traditional mingling of masquers and spectators. The effect in Beau-mont and Fletcher's play is quite different from that created in *Antonio's Revenge* and *The Revenger's Tragedy*, where the masque devotes itself entirely to the mingling of the masquers with their audience. The theater spectator's attention in those plays is strongly drawn both to the way the revels fulfills the specific purposes of its producers and to the response of the on-stage audience. The masque in *The Duchess of Malfi* shares more features with these than with the nuptial masque in *The Maid's Tragedy*. Though not a fatal masque, it is in many ways a revels of revenge, and it draws attention not primarily to its own features but to the purposes and projects of the character who instigates it, Ferdinand, and to the responses of its royal spectator, the Duchess herself.

The masque in *The Duchess of Malfi* is the madmen's interlude sent by Ferdinand to his sister just before Bosola comes to prepare her for death. It is the one masque of the six studied here that is not specifically labeled as a masque by a character in the play. Yet there exists adequate justification for admitting it to the company of other masques within plays.

There is a long critical habit of calling the madmen's visit a masque. Early in the nineteenth century, Charles Lamb spoke of "the wild masque of madmen,"[1] and many have followed his lead. Two decades ago, Inga-Stina Ekeblad [Ewbank] argued in some detail that all the features of the Elizabethan court masque are present in the scene and that the madmen's interlude constitutes an antimasque to the prolonged masque of death that follows.[2] There has been no strong challenge to the label since her article appeared.

But a critical tradition does not sufficiently warrant treating the sequence as a masque. I have suggested that we rely instead on a character's word, and at one moment Ferdinand supplies it. Before that moment, however, there is Ferdinand's early reference to masquery when he is warning the Duchess against a second marriage: "I would have you to give o'er these chargeable revels; / A visor and a mask are whispering-rooms / That were ne'er built for goodness" (1.1.333-35). In this passage the editor, John Russell Brown, has silently changed the quarto's "masque" to "mask." He does this at two other points in the play: once at 2.3.76 where the spelling is ascribed to a variant reading in Q4 rather than to modernization,[3] and again silently at 3.2.159 where the context, which refers to something worn, leaves no doubt as to which modern spelling is appropriate. Here in the first act, however, there is indeed some doubt, and Brown's silence is puzzling. Since a visor is so similar to a mask there is little point in the repetition, and Webster is not normally given to doublets. Moreover, the "revels" in the previous line argues by association for "masque" rather more than for "mask." In its dramatic context, with Ferdinand expressing an almost Supervacuous view of revels and visors just after showing the Duchess his father's poniard and just before offering that leering definition of the tongue as "that part which, like the lamprey, / Hath

ne'er a bone in't" (336-37), the word in both its senses is allied with
Ferdinand's distaste for his sister's conduct.

The same alliance is made in a speech of Ferdinand's shortly before the Duchess' death. After the nocturnal visit to his sister in which
he gives her a dead man's hand and shows her the wax figures of her husband and children, Ferdinand returns to Bosola. "Damn her!" he says,

> that body of hers,
> While that my blood ran pure in't, was more worth
> Than that which thou wouldst comfort, call'd a soul—
> I will send her masques of common courtesans,
> Have her meat serv'd up by bawds and ruffians,
> And, 'cause she'll needs be mad, I am resolv'd
> To remove forth the common hospital
> All the mad-folk, and place them near her lodging;
> There let them practise together, sing, and dance,
> And act their gambols to the full o'th' moon:
>
> (4.1.121-30)

The conjunction between sending masques of courtesans and sending mad-folk aligns them as alike serving Ferdinand's purposes.[4]
Since Ferdinand, who instigates the madmen's visit to the Duchess,
perceives that visit as a masque, or at the least as masque-like,
modern students of Webster's play are authorized to use the same
term Ferdinand does.[5]

Sending the madmen to his sister is an action taken by Ferdinand in order to elicit a very specific reaction in the Duchess:
"'cause she'll needs be mad." The dramatic impact of the masque
depends upon that action and its reaction far more than it depends
upon any extradramatic source or analogue. Students of Webster
have found episodes resembling his masque in earlier plays,[6] in
court antimasques,[7] in actual events of Webster's day,[8] and in folk
tradition. Ekeblad has been much admired[9] and twice reprinted for
showing that the masque of madmen in *The Duchess of Malfi* derives from the folk tradition of *charivari*, the antic or grotesque
dances performed before women who remarried or who made un-
popular or unequal matches.[10] In Ekeblad's view, Webster's Jacobean audience would have seen the masque of madmen as "a kind of
charivari put on to 'mock' the Duchess for her remarriage,"[11] as, in
other words, a grotesque and belated nuptial masque presented by

Ferdinand to his sister. Though widely cited, Ekeblad's suggestion is not universally accepted; the Revels editor, for example, has noted that "disorderly antimasques graced weddings of absolute propriety,"[12] and Ekeblad herself observes the similarities between the antics of Webster's madmen and those of Thomas Campion's "twelve Frantics" who "fell into a mad measure" in *The Lord's Masque*, which was performed on the night of the marriage between Princess Elizabeth and the Elector Palatine.[13] In addition, Ekeblad nowhere accounts for the difference between what she claims Ferdinand's purpose to be and what Ferdinand says his purpose is, nor does the *charivari* source explain why Ferdinand chose madmen over other grotesques or even the courtesans he explicitly mentions. It is certainly true that, as Robert W. Dent has copiously shown,[14] Webster borrowed; the central question here as elsewhere, however, is less whence Webster borrowed than what he did, dramatically, with the loan.

The dramatic sequence of events into which the masque of madmen fits moves from Ferdinand's speech to Bosola at the end of the first prison scene through the death of the Duchess. Its climax, which critics commonly refer to as the second prison scene (4.2), begins with an exchange between the Duchess and her waiting-woman, Cariola. This is followed by a servant's announcement that the madmen are coming, then by the arrival of the madmen themselves. Their masque is composed of a song, some clipped dialogue, and a dance. The remainder of the scene is designed by the disguised Bosola, who proceeds through roles as tomb-maker, as bellman, as singer, and as supervisor of the strangling of both the Duchess and Cariola. Toward the end of the scene, Ferdinand comes in, but it is only after he has left Bosola alone with the body that the Duchess at last dies. When Webster's audience next sees Ferdinand, he is quite mad.

Madness, then, is not only the hinge or invention of the masque but also a central feature in its aftermath. Moreover, madness figures significantly in one or two earlier scenes, long before Ferdinand tells Bosola that "'cause she'll needs be mad, I am resolv'd / To remove forth the common hospital / All the mad-folk, and place them near her lodging."

In fact, madness is invoked in Ferdinand's first response to the news that his sister has given birth. Confirming for Webster's audience the servant's belief that the Duke has been put "out of his wits"

(2.4.69), Ferdinand tells his brother the Cardinal that "I have this night digg'd up a mandrake. . . . / And I am grown mad with't" (2.5.1-2). A moment later, when the Duke suggests that "It is some sin in us, heaven doth revenge / By her," the Cardinal is amazed: "Are you stark mad?" (2.5.65-66). The intensity of Ferdinand's reaction, here measured against the calmer disgust of his brother, has been translated by three characters, including the Duke himself, as madness.

We see something of this madness, though it is not so termed, in Duke Ferdinand's next encounter with his sister Duchess. The beginning of his longest speech in this scene anticipates, as many have noted, his final madness, but it also vents his present passion:

> The howling of a wolf
> Is music to thee, screech-owl, prithee peace!
> Whate'er thou art, that hast enjoy'd my sister,—
> For I am sure thou hear'st me—for thine own sake
> Let me not know thee: I came hither prepar'd
> To work thy discovery, yet am now persuaded
> It would beget such violent effects
> As would damn us both:—
>
> (3.2.88-95)

When he does at last work the discovery, when Bosola adds the identity of the Duchess' husband (3.3.71) to the Duke's knowledge of her pregnancies and remarriage, the violent effects are immediate. The confiscation of her dukedom (3.4.31-33) follows hard upon the banishment of the Duchess and her family from Ancona (3.4.7.5-7, 3.4.27). Bosola comes for Antonio's "head" but is sent back alone (3.5.22-55), husband and wife say their farewells, and just as Antonio leaves Bosola returns with a guard to take the Duchess to prison in her palace. "With such a pity," she says with no little irony, "men preserve alive / Pheasants and quails, when they are not fat enough / To be eaten" (3.5.111-13).

The image of animals being fattened for the table is singularly apt, for the Arragonian brethren share with other Jacobean revengers, just or unjust, the habit of prefixing a suitable torture to the kill. The whole of the fourth act, in fact, is devoted to Ferdinand's several devices for fattening his sister and the Duchess' steadfast refusal to eat. Her last words before she is strangled will complete the simile: "Go tell my brothers, when I am laid out, / They then may feed in quiet" (4.2.236-37).

The strength of her endurance is proclaimed from the first by no less astute an observer than Bosola:

> She's sad, as one long us'd to't; and she seems
> Rather to welcome the end of misery
> Than shun it:—a behaviour so noble
> As gives a majesty to adversity;
>
> (4.1.3-6)

This "disdain," as Ferdinand calls it (12), is evident in the answer given by the Duchess to Bosola's "comfort" (18-20), but it is sorely tried by the fraternal visit that follows. Ferdinand means to torture, not to comfort, when he tells the Duchess, "I account it the honourabl'st revenge, / Where I may kill, to pardon" (32-33; cf. 3-5). But his sealed peace (43) is only a dead man's hand, and his comfort consists of a "sad spectacle" given, Bosola says, that the Duchess "may wisely cease to grieve / For that which cannot be recovered" (59-60). Henceforth the torture in pardon is exceeded by the torture simply in living: "That's the greatest torture souls feel in hell— / In hell: that they must live, and cannot die" (70-71). The Duchess repeats this lament a moment later when a servant enters for the sole purpose, apparently, of wishing her "long life" (92). She responds to this and to Bosola's first offers of pity with a string of curses that ends with her departure on this sententious couplet: "Go howl them this: and say I long to bleed: / It is some mercy, when men kill with speed" (109-10).

But there is no mercy yet from Ferdinand. The two prison scenes are bridged with that brief exchange between Ferdinand and Bosola in which the Duke announces his plan to remove the mad-folk from the common hospital "'cause she'll needs be mad." There are other announcements here too. An especially telling one is Ferdinand's answer to Bosola's plain question "Why do you do this?": "To bring her to despair" (116). The theological connotation in "despair" is brought out in Bosola's plea that Ferdinand "Send her a penitential garment to put on / Next to her delicate skin, and furnish her / With beads and prayer-books" (119-21), which in turn sets off Ferdinand's long "Damn her" speech. That speech ends with the Duke's assurance that Bosola's "work is almost ended" (132), a line which, together with Bosola's vow never to appear again to the

Duchess in his own shape (134), makes the show to come sound a little like those that Ariel produced for the men of sin in *The Tempest*. For Duke Ferdinand, however, there is little possibility that "The rarer action is / In virtue than in vengeance" (*Tmp.*, 5.1.27-28); on the contrary, the Duke of Calabria intends Bosola to "feed a fire, as great as my revenge, / Which ne'er will slack, till it have spent his fuel" (140-41).

The noise of the madmen is heard from the very start of the second prison scene. It is a nice (in the Elizabethan sense of that word) paradox for the Duchess that "nothing but noise and folly / Can keep me in my right wits, whereas reason / And silence make me stark mad" (4.2.5-7). To Webster's audience this must have suggested that Ferdinand might yet fail in his hope of bringing her to despair. On the other hand, perhaps reason and silence are what the Duchess wants:

> I am not mad yet, to my cause of sorrow.
> Th' heaven o'er my head seems made of molten brass,
> The earth of flaming sulphur, yet I am not mad:
> I am acquainted with sad misery,
> As the tann'd galley-slave is with his oar;
> Necessity makes me suffer constantly,
> And custom makes it easy—
>
>   (24-30)

This is not despair. Armed thus against madness, the Duchess may say at the approach of the madmen simply "Let them come in" (44).

The servant's catalogue of madmen warrants some scrutiny, for it "presents," in the technical sense, the masque. It is also the sole textual resource for editors who must assign speech headings to the madmen's lines. In the servant's words,

> There's a mad lawyer, and a secular priest,
> A doctor that hath forfeited his wits
> By jealousy; an astrologian
> That in his works said such a day o' th' month
> Should be the day of doom, and failing of't,
> Ran mad; an English tailor, craz'd i'th' brain
> With the study of new fashion; a gentleman usher
> Quite beside himself, with care to keep in mind
> The number of his lady's salutations,
> Or 'How do you', she employ'd him in each morning;
> A farmer too, an excellent knave in grain,
> Mad 'cause he was hinder'd transportation:

> And let one broker that's mad loose to these,
> You'd think the devil were among them.
>
> (45-58)

These are the *dramatis personae* in the masque, or rather—since the cast is mad, the music dismal, and the dance confused—the antic masque.

The masque sequence itself has three parts: song, dialogue, and dance. The song is about itself:

> O, let us howl, some heavy note,
>   Some deadly dogged howl,
> Sounding as from the threat'ning throat
>   Of beasts, and fatal fowl!
> As ravens, screech-owls, bulls, and bears,
>   We'll bill and bawl our parts,
> Till irksome noise have cloy'd your ears
>   And corrosiv'd your hearts.
>
> (61-67)[15]

This comes close to literalizing Ferdinand's earlier remark to his sister, "The howling of a wolf / Is music to thee, screech-owl."[16] The effect is indeed one of "irksome noise," not just here in the song but also in the forty or so lines of prose that follow.

Some mention must be made of the problems posed here by the speech headings, or rather by the lack of speech headings. In Q1 (1623), the first four of the eighteen madmen's speeches are labeled 1. Madman, 2. Madman, 3. Madman, and 4. Madman. The next four are numbered 1., 2., 1., 3., and the next eight numbered 1., 2., 3., 4., 1., 2., 3., 4. The final two speeches are given the numbers 3. and 4. Most editors have felt it necessary to substitute occupations, culled from the servant's list already quoted, for these numbers. There are two difficulties with such substitutions. First, although most editors do agree on assignments for the first four speeches (astrologer, lawyer, priest, doctor), they are not always in agreement on later speeches. Secondly, only the numbers one through four are used in the text, but there are eight madmen. Frank B. Fieler has gone to some lengths to "demonstrate on internal evidence that Webster intended more than four speakers—probably all eight madmen were to have lines—and that the speeches can be assigned in a manner which will make them consistent with the characters who are voicing them."[17] The editions of F. L. Lucas and Elizabeth

Brennan had used only the four roles indicated in the first four speeches, assigning headings to later speeches by number and ignoring inconsistencies. But John Russell Brown's Revels edition opts for retention of Q1's numbers. Brown suggests that "probably Webster numbered the speeches 1 to 4 in order to show where they begin and end, expecting the uncharacterized speeches to be allocated among the eight Madmen as the scene was elaborated in rehearsals. Or Crane may have tried to simplify Webster's arrangement when he prepared the printer's copy."[18] These are certainly feasible explanations, but even Brown neglects a simple point. Whatever the means by which the text came to have its uncharacterized headings, it duplicates the uncharacterized nature of the scene in performance. The confusion in the madmen's lines undermines attempts by the audience (as it has undermined attempts by the editors) to assign identities. The servant's individualized list of causes notwithstanding, madness in its effects is a great equalizer. The absence of names in the headings is, like the absence of names in the speeches, part of the madness, and perhaps we flirt with editorial madness if we seek too long for method in it.

The speeches themselves harp on themes familiar to the madmen's two spectators and to Webster's theater audience: secular, religious, and especially sexual corruption. William Archer was not wrong when he called this stuff "dismal nonsense,"[19] but he missed the dramatic point of its being so. The Duchess, for whom alone the song is sung, the speeches spoken, and the dance danced, is fortified against it all. She is neither mad nor despairing when we hear her next. After the dance, Bosola returns in the guise of an old man (114.2), the image of Chronos, almost as if in horrifying answer to the first madman's question, "Doomsday not come yet?" (73). To this apparition the Duchess responds with a simple question: "Is he mad too?" (115). And in the dialogue that follows, the Duchess' increasingly rhetorical interrogatives respond to Bosola's successive attempts to reduce her to a soul imprisoned in "fantastical puff-paste" (126) until they reach the dramatic climax of the simple declarative line that is, among other things, a response to Ferdinand's attempt to bring madness into Malfi:

> Hah, my tomb!
> Thou speak'st as if I lay upon my death-bed,
> Gasping for breath: dost thou perceive me sick?
> (116-18)

Thou art not mad, sure—dost know me?

(121)

Who am I?

(123)

Am I not thy duchess?

(134)

I am Duchess of Malfi still.

(142)

The primary dramatic function of the masque of madmen is to lend resonance to that last line. The madmen have gone mad in their occupations; the Duchess is Duchess still. Ferdinand holds up to his sister Duchess an image of what he would have her be, and she rejects the role. Critics are rightly wont to follow Ekeblad in noting how the death scene proper, with its disguised "presenter" Bosola, its gifts to the royal spectator of coffin, cords, and bell, and its song, serves as a kind of main masque to the madmen's antic masque or antemasque.[20] To this notion we may perhaps add a suggestion that the Duchess' conduct stands in the same relation to the madmen's interlude as masque to antimasque. The confusion and preposterous gesticulation (Jonson would say) contrast with the decorous dignity and nobility of the Duchess' final moments. The madmen's visit is not only, as others have suggested, an antemasque to the "masque" of death that follows, but also a true antimasque—in Jonson's sense of "a foil or false masque" presenting "a spectacle of strangeness" (Queens, 12,17)—to the royal bearing, quite without madness, of the Duchess herself. Moreover, this masque of madmen is, as Jonson said of his hags in relation to his queens, "not unaptly sorting with the current and whole fall of the device" (18-19), and the device, in this instance, is not just the Duchess' death scene but the entire play, which continues for another act.

A secondary dramatic function of the masque of madmen is to lend resonance, mostly of the ironic kind, to Ferdinand's madness. The wicked is snared in the work of his own hands: it is Ferdinand, not the Duchess, who will needs be mad. As Gunnar Boklund has observed, "the introduction of the lunatics powerfully suggests the ultimate disorder to which Ferdinand hopes to reduce his sister . . . with rigorous, nemesislike irony the schemer is made to go mad."[21]

Or, in the words of the proverb that provides Ferdinand with his last line, "Like diamonds, we are cut with our own dust."

Ferdinand's lycanthropia has correctly been linked to the bestial imagery and wolf howls of his speeches, and Bosola's, in earlier scenes. But his madness takes forms that the audience *sees* in addition to that one instance, necessarily only reported, in which

> One met the duke, 'bout midnight in a lane
> Behind Saint Mark's church, with the leg of a man
> Upon his shoulder; and he howl'd fearfully;
> Said he was a wolf, only the difference
> Was, a wolf's skin was hairy on the outside,
> His on the inside;
>
> (5.2.13-18)

But when Ferdinand actually appears, his lycanthropia evidently in its daytime remission, his madness is more reminiscent of the madmen he sent to his sister than of the wolves so often invoked in his sanity. The paean to solitude (5.2.30-31), his attempt to catch his shadow (31-41), the description of patience (45-51), and his parting remark that "you are all of you like beasts for sacrifice; there's nothing left of you, but tongue, and belly, flattery, and lechery" (80-82), all recall the short prose sentences, richly evoking corruption, of the madmen. The same may be said of Ferdinand's brief speeches in his two final appearances. The only exception is the last speech, when, as Bosola notes (5.5.69-70), lucidity returns to the Duke of Calabria: "My sister! O! my sister! there's the cause on't" (5.5.71).

I have called the masque of madmen in *The Duchess of Malfi* a revels of revenge. By that I mean that it is arranged, like the revenge revels in *Antonio's Revenge* or in *The Revenger's Tragedy*, in order to fulfill a character's wish to bring vengeance down upon its central spectator by turning spectator into victim. *The Duchess of Malfi* departs from those two plays, however, in so powerfully distinguishing a character's purpose from the playwright's purpose, from, that is, the actual dramatic effects of the masque sequence upon onstage and theater audiences. What Ferdinand intended is that the Duchess should go mad; what Webster achieves is admiration—in its old sense—for the Duchess' splendid sanity. Finally, the unjust revenger Ferdinand is figuratively—as Marston's Piero and

Tourneur's Supervacuo are literally—snared in his own masque, in (to remember the Psalmist yet once more) the work of his own hands.

Inga-Stina Ekeblad's essay on the Duchess' death brought our understanding of the madmen's interlude far beyond those confused and curiously haunted remarks in Welsford's *The Court Masque*, such as "the tortures Flamineo [*sic*] devises for his sister are wildly improbable and also disgusting."[22] Ekeblad brought us beyond Louis B. Wright's explanation that Ferdinand's purpose in sending the madmen was to keep the Duchess awake (*per* 4.1.131) while Webster's purpose was to furnish his audience with some comic entertainment.[23] She also brought us beyond Reed's explanation that although Webster's purpose was to heighten "the preternatural horror of the scene," his effect was to provide "a brief spell of comic relief, although of a definitely macabre sort."[24] Yet even Ekeblad, helpful though she is in comparison to her predecessors, relies on the medieval French *charivari* to explain the masque. "This product of Webster's grim comico-satirical strain," she says of the madmen's interlude, "is, of course, in terms of realistic plot totally out of place here."[25] When she does confront (in a footnote) Ferdinand's very simple and not at all *charivari*-like reason for sending the madmen, "'cause she'll needs be mad," Ekeblad writes that "this still does not explain why the scene was given just the form it has."[26] But "realistic plot" is a Pandora's box (realistic to whom?), and "why the scene was given just the form it has" a question that admits more than one answer. One possible reason why the scene was given the form it has is because it derives from folk and antimasque traditions; dramatic descendants of the *charivari* survived into seventeenth-century England. But another equally possible reason why the scene was given the form it has was to create specific dramatic effects, to elicit from the theater audience specific responses to Ferdinand's action, to the masque itself, to the Duchess' reaction as spectator, to Ferdinand's own madness. However closely related the masque of madmen may. be to dramatic precedents, to analogues from the court masque, to the *charivari*, it is far more closely related to the context in which it is fixed: the death of the Duchess of Malfi in particular and, in a larger sense, through the actions of madness elsewhere too, the entire play of *The Duchess of Malfi*.

7

Middleton's
Women Beware Women

When all four of the masquers who had purportedly come to celebrate his nuptials instead lie dead or dying before him, the Duke of Florence in Thomas Middleton's *Women Beware Women* gives voice to his confused astonishment: "I have lost myself in this quite" (5.2.142). But a moment later, after Hippolito has put a full stop to an explanation of this "wonder" by running upon a weapon's point, the Duke has found himself enough to see that "Upon the first night of our nuptial honours / Destruction plays her triumph, and great mischiefs / Mask in expected pleasures, 'tis prodigious!" (5.2.170-72). The nuptial masque in this play is deadly. In the study of it the critic may, as the Duke understandably does for a time, lose himself in it quite. He may conclude that the scene is "an exhibition of lunatic chaos"[1] or that "the only possible reaction from the audience is a horrified bewilderment allied to laughter."[2] Alternatively, the critic may pause, as the Duke does later, over the mischief of the masque, the way it defies expectations, especially the expectations the critic sees as having been set up by the first four acts. He may then find that the masque, though not wholly chaotic, is not at all a fit conclusion to the problems of the play, that it is "an embarrassment to the dramatist who did not treat it with respect,"[3] that it is a "failure" and a "preposterous" denouement

which "no amount of forced ingenuity or brilliant verse could save."[4]
He may then conclude that the masque is an afterthought, stuck onto
the play, as one master of similes suggests, "like a cantilevered portico."[5] Or, as a third option, the critic may accept the unexpected
appearance of the masque, welcoming this strange deus-ex-Middle-
ton in sympathy for a playwright backed into a corner ("it is hard to
see what other device short of sinking a ship or burning a house could
cause so many deaths in little more than two hundred lines"[6]) or by
adducing other cases of the *ars moriendi* run amok: "the context of
the play makes us accept it, much as we accept the spontaneous
combustion in *Bleak House*."[7] The critical literature provides a rich
lode of response to the masque that ends *Women Beware Women*,
richer, in fact, than the material on any other single masque within a
play. Yet in all this literature, in all the apologies for Middleton's
masque and in all the (more frequent) condemnations of it, there is a
curious shortage of analysis. There is no lack of explanations about
what Thomas Middleton was doing—or meant to do, or failed to
do—when he ended his play with this spectacular nuptial entertainment; what seems to be frequently missing is a dramatic analysis
of the way individual masques are designed by individual characters
for their individual revenges. Only by understanding first what it is
the characters are doing can we hypothesize about what it is the
playwright is doing—and whether he succeeds or fails.

There are a few extradramatic matters of some interest. In
placing *Women Beware Women* prior to *The Changeling*, I am
following a widely (though by no means universally) accepted chronology for which there is, unfortunately, very little firm evidence.[8]
Women Beware Women may have been written at any time between 1609, when one of its sources was published in Venice, and
1627, when Middleton died. The play has no stage history; its first
known professional performance was in 1962, although Nathaniel
Richards does write, in his commendatory verses to the octavo of
1657, "I that have seen 't can say, having just cause, / Never came
tragedy off with more applause." Scholars' assignments of dates for
the play range from Fleay's 1613 to Ribner's 1626 or 1627.[9] The
year with the largest following is that assigned in the *Annals*: 1621.
Most students of Middleton feel that the play belongs to this late
stage in the dramatist's career, and there is some favor for Baldwin
Maxwell's suggestion that Middleton gave his Duke's age as 55

(1.3.91) in order to flatter James, who turned 55 in June of 1621.[10]
The Changeling was licensed in 1622 for performance by Lady
Elizabeth's company at the Phoenix; the play was given at Whitehall for the court on the 4th of January 1624. It is impossible to say
with certainty which of the two tragedies was written first or which
was performed first. Fortunately, the present discussion of the
masques in these plays in no way depends upon establishing priority
in either composition or production. Their probable proximity is the
main point, and in placing one before the other I have simply
followed what has become fairly standard practice in dating Middleton's canon.

The fatal nuptial masque in *Women Beware Women* is not in
any of Middleton's known sources or analogues. Neither Malespini's
Ducento Novelle (1609) nor Moryson's *Itinerary* (written c. 1620)
ends its version of the Bianca Cappello story with a masque, nor is
there any such incident in the French source for the Isabella-Hippolito plot.[11] J. R. Mulryne, surveying Middleton's alterations and
additions to his sources, concludes that

> his boldest contribution, and the most characteristic, lies in those
> scenes that function in the play as symbolic happenings or sum-
> maries. The best-known is the chess-game scene, but others like
> Hippolito's dance with Isabella or the Ward's auction-ring appraisal
> of her, or the final masque itself, are wholly Middleton's invention,
> and contribute much to the process of transformation by which he
> gives ethical and even tragic significance to material that had pre-
> viously been no more than story-telling.[12]

The three scenes widely considered to be the play's most dramatically effective and memorable, the scenes where Middleton shows
his "unique power of constructing group scenes, in which a very
large number of people—virtually the whole cast—interact, take
cues from each other, clash and score off each other,"[13] are the chess
scene in the second act, the banquet scene set dead center in the
play, and the final masque. Not one of these is suggested in the
source material.

No fewer than eight of Middleton's plays contain masques or
formal plans for masques: *Your Five Gallants* (1605), *Michaelmas
Term* (1606), *No Wit, No Help Like a Woman's* (1613), *More
Dissemblers Besides Women* (1615), *Hengist, King of Kent, or The
Mayor of Queenborough* (1618), *The Old Law* (1618), *Women*

Beware Women, and *The Changeling*.[14] The masque that ends *Your Five Gallants* is the one most often compared to the masque that ends *Women Beware Women*.[15] But Burton Fishman, who has a lengthy chapter on the tragedy in his dissertation on fatal masques, sees a closer analogy in the false marriage masque of *No Wit, No Help Like a Woman's*, where "as is the case in *Women Beware*, the false marriage finds its analogue in a masque that is similarly out of joint."[16] Both these inserted masques do share a number of elements with that in *Women Beware Women*. The fact is, though, that similarities of one sort or another could be found between almost any two of Middleton's masques within plays, all of which depend to some extent on disguise, on show, on "falseness." More significant than analogies is simply the volume of masques written by Middleton for plays prior to *Women Beware Women*. The nuptial entertainment in that tragedy is not the work of a playwright unfamiliar with the genre.

Middleton also wrote at least three court masques. His lost *Masque of Cupid* was performed at the Merchant Taylors' Hall in January of 1614 for the Earl of Somerset's wedding.[17] *The Inner Temple Masque, or Masque of Heroes*, was performed in 1619, about two years before the conjectured date of *Women Beware Women*.[18] *The World Tossed at Tennis*, written in collaboration with Rowley and performed about a year after *Heroes*, seems, according to Welsford, "to have been the first masque composed for the theater."[19] Welsford is slightly misleading: the title page announces that the masque was "prepared for his Majesties Entertainment at Denmarke-House," but it was not given there (for reasons unknown) and was apparently then modified for public performance.[20] The work as we now have it is a curious hybrid, neither pure masque nor pure play. Welsford correctly notes that "the plan prefixed to the libretto shows that if the piece differs from an ordinary play it differs still more from an ordinary masque."[21] The Prologue and Epilogue admit as much: "This our device we do not call a play"; "We must confess that we have vented ware / Not always vendible: masques are more rare / Than plays are common."[22] Only a year or two before the probable date of *Women Beware Women*, then, a London theater audience saw its first genuine intended-for-court masque (or masque *manqué*). Naturally, though, as prologue and epilogue show, "the players were fearful of

the success of this courtly innovation in the theater, as well they
might have been, for they were asking for comparison with spectacles whose brilliance they could not possibly approach."[23]

There remain a pair of distant but intriguing analogues to the
masque in *Women Beware Women*. One, to which attention is
drawn in a tantalizingly unelaborated footnote in Ewbank's study of
masques within plays, is the dumb show presented by Revenge to
Don Andrea in *The Spanish Tragedy*. As Revenge describes it,

> The two first, the nuptial torches bore,
> As brightly burning as the mid-day's sun:
> But after them doth Hymen hie as fast,
> Clothed in sable, and a saffron robe,
> And blows them out and quencheth them with blood,
> As discontent that things continue so.
>
> (3.15.30-35)

Ewbank writes that the masque in *Women Beware Women* "is a
working-out in masque and dramatic terms" of this show.[24] Revenge's conceit, in which blood quenches the nuptial torches, appears two decades or so later in Beaumont and Fletcher's tragicomedy *Philaster*, probably performed about 1609 by the King's
Men and printed in 1622. Towards the end of this play there is a
moment when Bellario, in Hymeneal robe and garland, presents the
wedded Arethusa and Philaster to her father the King. The King is
furious:

> Your dear husband! Call in
> The captain of the citadel; there you shall keep
> Your wedding! I'll provide a masque shall make
> Your Hymen turn his saffron into a sullen coat
> And sing sad requiems to your departing souls;
> Blood shall put out your torches, and instead
> Of gaudy flowers about your wanton necks
> An axe shall hang like a prodigious meteor,
> Ready to crop your loves' sweets.[25]

It is of course quite unlikely that these passages in much earlier
plays are sources for Middleton's blood-quenched nuptial masque;
some elements, like Hymen's saffron robe, are iconographic com-
monplaces (cf. *Hymenaei*, 42-45). But the commonness itself is interesting: the recurrence of yellow-robed Hymen, nuptial torches,

and fires quenched by blood (*Women Beware Women*, 5.2.50.1, 73.1-5, 149) suggests that Middleton's deadly nuptial masque is iconographically akin to these other emblems of vengeance on ill-conceived marriages.

The masque in *Women Beware Women* fuses several separate plots.[26] There is Bianca's "antemasque" in which she attempts to kill the Cardinal and instead poisons the Duke. The main masque— in which Juno resolves the troubles of the nymph who has two lovers and in which the rejected lover is supposed to raise Slander— harbors no fewer than four deadly plans. Guardiano has the trapdoor and galtrop for Hippolito, Isabella has the poisoned incense for Livia, Livia has a murderous "take that" for Isabella (perhaps a shower of flaming gold[27]), and Guardiano—who has fallen through his own trapdoor and thus needs his alternate plan—has Cupids with poisoned arrows who shoot at Hippolito. The sixth death in the scene is Bianca's suicide, which though not part of the antemasque or masque is a dramaturgically inevitable reaction to them. Bianca's death is the sole event that might not have been foreseen by Middleton's theater audience at the start of the masque. Everything else is either plotted in the audience's hearing beforehand (plus or minus the details) or—in the case of Bianca's poisoned cups—explained in asides at the time. The reactions of the Duke and Fabritio to departures from the masque's argument therefore cannot duplicate the reactions of the knowing audience any more than, for example, the Spanish King's shock at the deaths in Hieronimo's "Soliman and Perseda" can duplicate the reaction of an audience that saw them coming. The dramatic effect of the masque in *Women Beware Women* resides not in the individual death plots but in the ways they are knit together into a whole. In order to study the weave, however, one must first isolate the strands that compose it.

One such strand belongs to Guardiano. Guardiano's double plot against Hippolito (galtrop backed up by poisoned arrows) is as revenge for damage done to Isabella, whom Guardiano had hoped to wed to his Ward. When Livia, in the violence of her reaction to Leantio's death, taunts Hippolito with "the black lust 'twixt thy niece and thee" (4.2.66), Guardiano takes the revelation as a personal dishonor (4.2.76-78) and vows that "I'll list to nothing but revenge and anger, / Whose counsels I will follow" (4.2.93-94).

When he next appears, Guardiano has hit upon the occasion for his revenge:

> As I can wear my injuries in a smile,
> Here's an occasion offered that gives anger
> Both liberty and safety to perform
> Things worth the fire it holds, without the fear
> Of danger, or of law; for mischiefs acted
> Under the privilege of a marriage-triumph
> At the Duke's hasty nuptials, will be thought
> Things merely accidental—all 's by chance,
> Not got of their own natures.
>
> (4.2.158-66)

Guardiano and Livia join forces now against Hippolito as they had earlier joined their wits and their ambitions in procuring Bianca for the Duke. The arrows that eventually hit Hippolito are Guardiano's idea, but the pages who shoot them are Livia's followers. The trapdoor for the galtrop is Guardiano's own device. Like the place at the end of the parlor where Leantio wants to hide Bianca (3.2.162-67) or the argument of the masque itself, this trapdoor has a history. The Ward, who is to handle the machinery during the masque, knows it "of old, uncle, since the last triumph; here rose up a devil with one eye, I remember, with a company of fireworks at 's tail" (5.1.7-9). The poetic justice with which Guardiano will fall through his own devilish door needs no belaboring here. There is less blatant irony in the confidence and security with which he goes about arranging his overkill:

> If this should any way miscarry now,
> As, if the fool be nimble enough, 'tis certain,
> The pages that present the swift-winged Cupids
> Are taught to hit him with their shafts of love
> (Fitting his part) which I have cunningly poisoned.
> He cannot 'scape my fury; and those ills
> Will be laid all on fortune, not our wills.
> That's all the sport on 't; for who will imagine,
> That at the celebration of this night
> Any mischance that haps can flow from spite?
>
> (5.1.30-39)

For a theater audience so thoroughly informed about the trapdoor

and its concealed galtrop, the surprise is not in the fall itself—as it is
for the Duke—but in the identity of the actual victim.

The vengeance most closely allied to Guardiano's is Livia's.
The two have been paired in mischief since their excellent work on
Leantio's mother and wife—"it's a witty age" (2.2.396) indeed—in
the chess scene that so impressed T. S. Eliot. Now they share a
hatred of Hippolito, and Livia vows full vengeance for Leantio's
death in terms as plain as Guardiano's (4.2.233-34). But her role in
the masque is larger than his. For one thing, the production is her
idea, even though its argument is not her invention:

> This gentleman [Guardiano] and I had once a purpose
> To have honoured the first marriage of the Duke
> With an invention of his own; 'twas ready,
> The pains well past, most of the charge bestowed on 't,
> Then came the death of your good mother, niece,
> And turned the glory of it all to black.
> 'Tis a device would fit these times so well too,
> Art's treasury not better; if you'll join
> It shall be done, the cost shall all be mine.
>
> (4.2.202-10)

There are intriguing details here: the Duke's first marriage, the
untimely end of Isabella's mother ("a lady who, like Leantio's father
and Bianca's parents, is more present in the play than the cast-list
would suggest"[28]), a nuptial entertainment postponed by the intrusion of death, the delicate irony in " 'Tis a device would fit these
times so well too." There is an ambiguity in the "his" of the excerpt's
third line; Mulryne writes "probably Guardiano's; the Duke's, possibly, making for an even more ironic outcome."[29] The stress on
"own" makes the Duke a likely inventor, but that reading would
make his later reliance on the masque's argument rather puzzling.
Mulryne's "probably Guardiano's" is borne out by Guardiano's familiarity with the plot (4.2.213-28; cf. 5.2.163). The especially
interesting thing about this speech of Livia's is the trouble taken to
give the masque a history, an origin. Hieronimo does this too when
he begins, "When in Toledo there I studied, / It was my chance to
write a tragedy" (*The Spanish Tragedy*, 4.1.77-78). One effect
certainly is, as Ewbank notes, "a sense of continuous life."[30] But in
The Spanish Tragedy Hieronimo's "Soliman and Perseda" is a
command performance, not his own idea; here in *Women Beware*

Women Livia and Guardiano are, as Balthazar is in Kyd's play, caught in a net of their own making. There is, of course, a good deal of anticipatory irony in her "the cost shall all be mine."

Livia is not seen again until she descends as Juno Pronuba, the marriage goddess. The appropriateness of that role to Livia, procuress for the Duke, Hippolito, and (by offering herself) Leantio, has been observed in nearly every comment on the masque since Bradbrook's.[31] But few also comment on the blazing *doubles entendres* when Livia-as-Juno says to Isabella-as-Nymph, "Though you and your affections / Seem all as dark to our illustrious brightness / As night's inheritance hell, we pity you" (5.2.104-06). These affections, Isabella's for Hippolito, are the object of Livia's wrath now. It is Isabella, who had no direct hand in the murder of Leantio, the murder which Livia is so determined to avenge, who receives Juno's "token": "Now for a sign of wealth and golden days, / Bright-eyed prosperity which all couples love, / Ay, and makes love, take that—" (5.2.115-17). Isabella falls, not Hippolito. For Middleton's theater audience, the unexpected event is not the murder itself, but, once more, the identity of the victim.

There is no surprise at all in Isabella's victim. The progress toward her vengeance begins in the aftermath of Livia's revelation that Isabella is in fact Hippolito's niece. She is speaking now only for the theater audience:

> Was ever maid so cruelly beguiled
> To the confusion of life, soul, and honour,
> All of one woman's murd'ring! I'd fain bring
> Her name no nearer to my blood than woman,
> And 'tis too much of that. Oh shame and horror!
> In that small distance from yon man to me
> Lies sin enough to make a whole world perish.
> (4.2.129-35)

She turns to her uncle then and banishes him from her sight. Turning back to the audience, Isabella makes her intentions quite clear:

> But for her
> That durst so dally with a sin so dangerous,
> And lay a snare so spitefully for my youth,
> If the least means but favour my revenge,
> That I may practise the like cruel cunning

> Upon her life, as she has on mine honour,
> I'll act it without pity.
>
> (4.2.144-50)

The only element unforeseen by the theater audience when Isabella does act against Livia in the masque is in the means of death, the poisoned incense. And that, for the audience's sake, is glossed in an aside:

> I offer to thy powerful deity
> This precious incense; may it ascend peacefully—
> [Aside] And if it keep true touch, my good aunt Juno,
> 'Twill try your immortality ere 't be long,
> I fear you'll never get so nigh heaven again,
> When you're once down.
>
> (5.2.99-104)

Since Hippolito, although threatened by both a galtrop and poisoned arrows, has no murderous plot of his own in the masque, there remains only Bianca's "antemasque."

The scene had begun with an apparent reconciliation between Bianca, now Duchess, and the Duke's brother the Lord Cardinal. But just when peace between the two seems sealed, Bianca has this aside: "Cardinal, you die this night, the plot's laid surely— / In time of sports death may steal in securely, / Then 'tis least thought on" (5.2.21-23). Bianca is the second confident plotter to observe that revels are murder's license (cf. 4.2.161-66, 5.1.35-39).

The masque sequence itself, for which the theater audience is by now quite thoroughly prepared, begins with the Duke reading the argument. For the theater audience this is the second summary of the masque's "invention." Music announces an entry, but instead of nymphs and shepherds the spectators are greeted by Hymen, Ganymede, and Hebe. Hymen gives Bianca a cup, and Hebe delivers cups to the Duke and the Cardinal. The stage direction supplied here—"To the Duke the wrong cup by mistake"—comes from an annotation in a seventeenth-century hand in Yale's copy of the octavo.[32] Though a theater audience cannot know yet that the wrong cup has been given, or even that there is a right cup and a wrong cup, some spectators would surely have been alerted by the strange exchange between Hebe and Ganymede, with its references to stumbling, to cups spilled and stolen. More telling is the way

Bianca explains away the whole event, which we should remember is as much a surprise to the theater audience as it is to the on-stage audience, as "some antemasque belike, my lord, / To entertain time. Now my peace is perfect, / Let sports come on apace" (5.2.69-71). "Peace" is picked up from the peace she had sealed earlier with the Cardinal, and "sports" echoes "In time of sports death may steal in securely." The attentive listener cannot miss the implications.

Music sounds again, and this time the promise of the argument is fulfilled by the entrance of Isabella and two nymphs. The masque proceeds as intended now with a song, Isabella's invocation to Juno, the entry of Hippolito and Guardiano as shepherds, and the descent of Livia-Juno. There are brief asides from Isabella and Livia which alert the audience to the fact that the incense is poisoned, but it is not until Isabella falls down upon Livia's "take that" that the on-stage spectators, chiefly the Duke and Fabritio, note anything amiss. This first departure from the argument is quickly followed by a second (Guardiano's fall), and while Fabritio finds both developments quite consistent with the masque's conceit, the Duke is less tolerant. With Isabella and Guardiano already dispatched, Livia casts aside her part as Juno to say:

> Oh I am sick to th' death, let me down quickly;
> This fume is deadly. Oh 't has poisoned me!
> My subtlety is sped, her art has quitted me;
> My own ambition pulls me down to ruin.
>
> (5.2.130-33)

But there is some indication that the on-stage audience does not hear Livia's dying words; Fabritio's confusion (135-38) makes little sense otherwise. He and the Duke do not begin to see what has happened until Hippolito, mortally wounded, calls for the Cupids' capture (140-41) and begins to explain to his royal audience, "My great lords, we are all confounded" (143).

Of the four masquers only Hippolito now remains alive. His explanation of the events must therefore be comprehensive, as indeed it is:

> Lust and forgetfulness has been amongst us,
> And we are brought to nothing. Some blest charity
> Lend me the speeding pity of his sword

To quench this fire in blood. Leantio's death
Has brought all this upon us—now I taste it—
And made us lay plots to confound each other.
The event so proves it, and man's understanding
Is riper at his fall than all his life-time.
She in a madness for her lover's death
Revealed a fearful lust in our near bloods,
For which I am punished dreadfully and unlooked for;
Proved her own ruin too: vengeance met vengeance
Like a set match, as if the plagues of sin
Had been agreed to meet here altogether.
But how her fawning partner fell I reach not,
Unless caught by some springe of his own setting;
For, on my pain, he never dreamed of dying,
The plot was all his own, and he had cunning
Enough to save himself—but 'tis the property
Of guilty deeds to draw your wise men downward.
Therefore the wonder ceases.

                                            (5.2.146-66)

For the Duke, who has not the benefit of the theater audience's
knowledge, this speech gives the essential facts about Livia, Guardiano, and Hippolito himself. Isabella has been pronounced dead
already (144) and is of course implicated in her uncle's "fearful lust in
our near bloods." Only Bianca's plot now remains incomplete—and
yet unconfounded.

After hearing this speech the Duke can obviously no longer be
lost "in this quite." He indicates as much when he observes that
"Upon the first night of our nuptial honours / Destruction plays her
triumph, and great mischiefs / Mask in expected pleasures"
(170-72). But he continues in a different vein, turning from what is
past to what is to come: " 'tis prodigious! / They're things most
fearfully ominous, I like 'em not" (172-73). What is noteworthy here
is the Duke's sense of fright, almost like Antonio in *The Revenger's
Tragedy* saying "You that would murder him would murder me."
But this Duke's fear is warranted: a moment later he sickens.
Recognizing now what some members of the theater audience may
have suspected, that "My deadly hand is fallen upon my lord" (185),
Bianca drinks from the errant cup. As Hippolito had before her, she
remembers in the moment of death the one person who has unwittingly set in motion all the events of the masque: "Leantio, now I
feel the breach of marriage / At my heart-breaking" (210-11). After

that there is only a litany of maxims ending with the Cardinal's sententious quatrain:

> Sin, what thou art these ruins show too piteously.
> Two kings on one throne cannot sit together,
> But one must needs down, for his title's wrong;
> So where lust reigns, that prince cannot reign long.
>
> (5.2.222-25)

The copy for the single early text of *Women Beware Women*, the 1657 octavo *Two New Playes*, probably did not originate in the theater. The sparseness of stage directions is felt most keenly in this last act; Mulryne notes with some frustration that "the octavo hardly does justice however to Middleton's intentions for the masque."[33] But Middleton's intentions never were available to us and the circumstances of early performances—if indeed there were early performances—are lost in theatrical history. On the other hand, I have tried to show that the text itself is not only an adequate guide to the actions and reactions of masquers and on-stage spectators but is also a guide—and, however imperfect, the only guide—to possible reactions of a Jacobean theater audience.

Analysis of the masque scene points toward conclusions rather different from those that have been reached by some of Middleton's best critics. R. B. Parker cannot be right when he justifies his claim that "the only possible reaction from the audience is a horrified bewilderment allied to laughter" by saying that "such effect seems to have been intended by Middleton, at least in part, because he arranges that the inevitable confusion of the audience is shared, formulated, and thus confirmed, by the remarks of Fabritio and the Duke, onlookers at the masque who cannot understand what is happening."[34] The audience's confusion can only be inevitable if we strip from the text all the prior planning and asides of those characters involved in the masque.

The frequently encountered objection that the masque is somehow a violation of the "realism" or "naturalism" of the preceding four acts is hardly tenable either. For one thing, a masque was for Middleton's audience no more "unrealistic" than a royal marriage; Ewbank is quite right to see that "the masque is as natural a form of social occasion in the world of the play as is the ball in *The Cherry Orchard* or the coffee-party in *Pillars of Society*."[35] And the vindictive plots that are carried out under cover of the masque are no more "unrealistic" than the events that led to them: Hippolito's murder of Leantio, the incest between Isabella and her uncle, the ease with which Bianca succumbs to the Duke and rejects her husband.

It is only the cumulative effect of so many plots coming together at once ("as if the plagues of sin / Had been agreed to meet here altogether") and of so many plots falling down upon the inventors' heads ("My own ambition pulls me down to ruin") that comes unexpectedly to the theater spectators. But those are the very things that also come unexpectedly to the conspirators. Audience reaction is, then, comparable not to the inevitable confusion of the Duke and Fabritio but rather to the realizations of the dying masquers and the ruined Bianca, all of whose vengeful plans the theater audience has foreknown. Those realizations are variations on an invariable theme: Livia's "My own ambition pulls me down to ruin," Guardiano being "caught by some springe of his own setting," Hippolito hastening his own death, Bianca's suicide as she says to the Duke "Thus, thus, reward thy murderer," an unnamed Lord noting "What shift sh' has made to be her own destruction." The theme should be familiar; we have seen it in the entertainments in *The Spanish Tragedy*, *Antonio's Revenge*, *The Revenger's Tragedy*, and *The Duchess of Malfi*. It is nothing very much more complex than the well-worn Psalm 9:16 glossing another inserted masque. What Middleton has done—and herein resides the great dramatic power of the scene—is to work out of a singularly appropriate masque not one or two or three but six dramatic instances of the wicked being snared in the masque of his or her own hands.

8

Middleton and Rowley's
The Changeling

There is no masque in *The Changeling*. But neither is there a
marriage for a masque to celebrate. The marriage of Beatrice to
Alonzo never takes place, the marriage of Beatrice to Alsemero is
never consummated, and the dance that Alibius is asked to produce
for the third night's nuptial revels is planned and rehearsed but
never performed before its intended audience. Yet the preparations
for the masque are as important in the subplot as the preparations
for marriage are in the main plot.

The several actions and speeches pertaining to Beatrice's nuptial entertainment in *The Changeling* can only be treated in connection with the much larger issue of the link between the two plots and
with the much hazier issue of the text. The pertinence of both these
issues is readily apparent in those two scenes in which plans for the
nuptial revels dominate the dramatic action.

The first of these scenes begins when the doctor Alibius brings
news to his man Lollio:

> We have employment, we have task in hand;
> At noble Vermandero's, our castle-captain,
> There is a nuptial to be solemnis'd
> (Beatrice-Joanna, his fair daughter, bride),
> For which the gentleman hath bespoke our pains:

> A mixture of our madmen and our fools,
> To finish, as it were, and make the fag
> Of all the revels, the third night from the first;
> Only an unexpected passage over,
> To make a frightful pleasure, that is all,
> But not the all I aim at; could we so act it,
> To teach it in a wild distracted measure,
> Though out of form and figure, breaking time's head,
> It were no matter, 'twould be heal'd again
> In one age or other, if not in this:
> This, this, Lollio, there's a good reward begun,
> And will beget a bounty, be it known.
>
>   (3.3.251-67)

To that speech Lollio replies,

> This is easy, sir, I'll warrant you: you have about you fools and
> madmen that can dance very well; and 'tis no wonder, your best
> dancers are not the wisest men; the reason is, with often jumping they
> jolt their brains down into their feet, that their wits lie more in their
> heels than in their heads.
>
>   (3.3.268-73)

Isabella is present during this exchange, but she merely remarks the more practical side of the venture: "Madmen and fools are a staple commodity" (3.3.276). The "frightful pleasure" bespoken is intended by Vermandero for his daughter's wedding to Alonzo, whom the theater audience has just seen De Flores kill. The entertainment described by Alibius as "the all I aim at" belongs, as William Empson and others since him have observed, to the antic masque tradition (since it is "to close up the solemnity" [4.3.54] it is more a postmasque than an antemasque). Empson wrote:

> The antimasque at a great wedding, considered as subhuman, stood
> for the insanity of disorder to show marriage as necessary, considered
> as the mob ritually mocked the couple (for being or for not being
> faithful, innocent, etc.), both to appease those who might otherwise
> mock and to show that the marriage was too strong to be hurt by
> mockery.[1]

As a "wild distracted measure" to be performed at a wedding, the planned dance of madmen and fools clearly belongs with the rebellion of the humors and affections in *Hymenaei* or the "mad measure" of the twelve frantics in Campion's *The Lords' Masque*. From

Alibius' brief description, this dance will fit Jonson's definition of an antimasque: "not as a masque but a spectacle of strangeness, producing multiplicity of gesture" (*Queens*, 17-18). Ekeblad might call it a *charivari*, especially since the main plot's marriage is defiled.

The second scene in which this nuptial entertainment figures comes an act later, just after the newly married Beatrice has passed her virginity test and just before the final rush of events at the castle. Lollio reports on the progress of preparations for the "madmen's morris" (4.3.65), which he mistrusts (56), and for the "whole measure" (68). Alibius asks for one more rehearsal (64). But before this dance of madmen and fools, there are four brief events, each of which contains important suggestions as to its staging. In one, Antonio goes through the dance Lollio has taught him (82-101). In the next, Isabella comes to Antonio in her madwoman's disguise but leaves "stark mad" when the "fool"—here truly foolish—fails to recognize her. In the third and fourth, Lollio, like the Vice Ambidexter and his many dramatic ancestors and heirs, sets Antonio and Franciscus, rivals for Isabella's favors, against each other. First Lollio tells the counterfeit fool Antonio,

> come, I can give you comfort; my mistress loves you, and
> there is as arrant a madman i' th' house as you are a fool, your rival,
> whom she loves not; if after the masque we can rid her of him, you
> earn her love, she says, and the fool shall ride her.
>
> (4.3.147-51)

Antonio immediately assures Lollio that "She's eas'd of him; I have a good quarrel on't" (154). Lollio uses the same technique on the counterfeit madman Franciscus, who likewise assures the doctor's man that any enemy of Isabella's is "dead already!" (191-92). The hot lover is reminded to "see him before you kill him" (195) and told, "Only reserve him till the masque be past, and if you find him not now in the dance yourself, I'll show you" (201-02). Each rival is committed to removing the other from Isabella's way after the masque. His work done, Lollio presents for Alibius and Isabella the dance of madmen and fools, which is pronounced by the doctor to be "perfect" (213).

These are the two scenes in *The Changeling* that are concerned with Beatrice's nuptial revels. In the final act the characters from the subplot join the characters from the main plot only twice: when

Alibius and Isabella tell the revenger Tomazo that the suspected murderers may be found in disguise at the hospital (5.2.49-87) and in the final scene (5.3.121-219). In neither of these is Lollio or the well-rehearsed dance of madmen and fools mentioned. The masque referred to twice by Lollio is never performed before its intended audience.

More than one critic has sensed textual corruption in all this. E.H.C. Oliphant is the first and Richard Levin the most recent to posit a missing scene. Introducing his edition of *The Changeling*, Oliphant wrote,

> It seems likely that in the original version there was at least one scene in which Antonio and Franciscus arranged to become counterfeit inmates of Alibius's institution for the insane; as it is, Antonio is introduced in I 2 without any preparation; and the introduction of Franciscus in III 3 leaves even more to be desired. In IV 3 we have careful preparation for a masque at the castle of Vermandero; but it comes to nought: it seems probable that Rowley's intentions in this matter were not realized. Probably Middleton's ideas were different and prevailed.[2]

But N.W. Bawcutt, editing *The Changeling* in 1958 for the then-new Revels series, demurred on both points. Bawcutt wrote that a scene introducing Isabella's two suitors "is hardly necessary" and that "the dance of fools and madmen at the end of IV.iii does away with the need for a scene which would have been very difficult to fit in to the later part of the play."[3]

While the lack of a scene introducing Antonio and Franciscus bothered no one but Oliphant, the unperformed nuptial entertainment continued to trouble critics. In the present decade, Dorothy Farr has tried to deal with Oliphant's objections, and some others of her own, without recourse to a lost-scene theory:

> My own impression is that Rowley was working in close association with Middleton in the passages concerned with the madmen, but that, either in the harassment of completing the play to meet a demand, or in revising it for a Court performance, hasty modifications were made, perhaps during the process of writing.[4]

"Hasty modifications" are, however, less satisfying as a proposed solution—assuming one perceives a problem—than a lost scene, since the rest of the text gives little evidence of either haste or modification.

Two years before Farr's book appeared (though apparently too late for her to consult), Richard Levin had published a study of double and multiple plots. Levin reverts to the lost-scene theory espoused by Oliphant, but he avoids the earlier critic's talk of dramatists' "intentions" by confining himself to the logic of the plot. Levin's argument is important and attractive enough to warrant quoting at some length:

> For we are missing a major scene, just before or in place of the present V.ii, which was carefully prepared for to bring this action to its climax and into direct contact with the main plot. Presumably it would be set in the castle and would show the wedding masque, rehearsed in IV.iii, that imports "madness" into this world, then the fight between Antonio and Franciscus over Isabella, also arranged in IV.iii to follow after "the masque be past," during which these two counterfeits would give away their identities to the stage audience (including Alibius, who would thereby learn how his jealous imprisonment of Isabella had almost made him a cuckold), and then their arrest for Alonzo's murder. This would provide not only the much needed comic deflations of Antonio, Franciscus, and Alibius, the absence of which leaves us perplexed and frustrated (the perfunctory confession of their "changes" in the closing lines of the play is certainly no substitute for the dramatization of them, and in fact seems to look back to such a dramatization), but also a much better discovery scene for this plot than V.ii now gives us, since there is no reason why Isabella should have told Alibius about her suitors before the masque. And this scene might also have affected the main plot as well. The public arrest of Antonio and Franciscus could make Beatrice and De Flores feel more secure (in our version they are not even aware that these men are suspected of their crime), and so more careless, thus increasing the probability of Alsemero's coming upon them in the incident reported at the beginning of V.iii. . . . The present V.ii seems a clumsy piece of patchwork covering up a missed opportunity to bring the two plots together on the stage in a climactic interaction . . . that would have reinforced the moral contrast basic to their formal integration.[5]

Dangerous though it may be to "improve" Renaissance plays in this fashion, Levin does raise objections that are not easily ignored and does propose a solution that cannot be blithely dismissed. His theory might even be buttressed by observing that this "missed opportunity" to join plots "in a climactic interaction" is precisely the scene that is so effectively *not* missing from *Women Beware Women*.

But there, perhaps, is a rub. Would playwrights so given to inserting a masque within a play have planned but then for some reason failed to write one, as Levin suggests?[6] Or if such a scene was actually written, was it likely to have been lost[7] (and the loss not noted for three centuries) in the thirty years between compositon and publication, when for twenty of those years the play was often acted and when even the closing of the theaters failed to diminish its popularity?[8] Perhaps there is no "missed opportunity" at all. Perhaps the dance and its attendant business are something more, or at least something other, than merely a promise of an incident that never materializes.

There is one quite obvious function of the dance in *The Changeling*: it is a direct link between the subplot and the main plot. Characters from Alibius' hospital are asked to supply an entertainment for characters in Vermandero's household. Many both before and after Empson have noted this, but Richard Levin must be credited with showing how this "causal" or "efficient" connection ("in which a character or event from one line of action directly affects the other"[9]) differs from other, less obvious, links between the plots. The richest of those other connections, the one Empson first described, is what Levin calls "formal": "the two parallel 'ratios'—Beatrice : Alonzo : Alsemero : De Flores ~ Isabella : Alibius : Antonio and Franciscus : Lollio."[10] But if these ratios are as pervasively operative in the play as Levin and others claim, then they ought to be operative in and through the rehearsed wedding entertainment as well as in and through character, thought, diction, or imagery. And if the ratio does operate in and through the scene, then the dance of fools and madmen is something more "formal," in Levin's sense, than just an "efficient" connection that is never quite fully made.

De Flores' counterpart in the subplot is widely acknowledged to be Lollio. Empson wrote of the "striking parallel between De Flores and the subordinate keeper Lollio, who has some claim to be counted among the fools. He demands 'his share' from Isabella as a price for keeping his mouth shut about Antonio, just as De Flores does from Beatrice."[11] Bradbrook noted that Isabella's reply to Lollio's overtures (3.3.240-44) shares a reference to cut throats with the service De Flores does Beatrice.[12] Karl Holzknecht neatly summed up the parallels by saying that what Lollio demands of Isabella—"My share, that's all" (3.3.245)—"is all De Flores had demanded of Bea-trice Joanna."[13] But Lollio is quite content to get his "share" by means other than eliminating his rivals Antonio and Franciscus or Isabella's jealous husband Alibius: "I put in for my thirds," he says, "I shall be mad or fool else" (4.3.36-37). The ones who threaten not to be content with "thirds," or even seconds, are Antonio and Fran-ciscus. When Lollio arranges for each to do battle with the other after the masque, the echo of De Flores is heard not from the doctor's man but from Antonio and Franciscus. Antonio is quite confident that "She's eas'd of him; I have a good quarrel on 't" (4.3.154). Franciscus' vow is rasher: "He's dead already!" (192). That vow is far more serious, more reminiscent of De Flores' "I thirst for him" or "His end's upon him; / He shall be seen no more" (2.2.133-35), than Lollio's suggestion that the counterfeit madman "bang but his fool's coat well-favouredly" (4.3.198).

This is not to suggest that the Lollio-De Flores term of the ratio is not powerfully operative; on the contrary, it is second in signifi-cance only to the Isabella-Beatrice term. I wish merely to submit that the subplot-main plot ratio is not so neat and binding as to exclude briefly suggested but powerfully ominous links between Antonio and De Flores and, more tightly still, between Franciscus and De Flores.

For the dance itself the quarto of 1653 provides the barest of stage directions: "The Madmen and Fools dance" (4.3.212.2). But additional bits of significant information can be extrapolated from the text. Lollio quite clearly acts as presenter of work that is essen-tially his own choreographed creation (207, 211). Alibius is not the only spectator, for Isabella is specifically entreated by Lollio, at her husband's request, "to see this sight" (208). If an earlier description of the madmen as birds and beasts (3.3.190.1) applies to costume, the madmen may be similarly clothed here; if the description refers to imitative actions, the madmen may deal similarly here.

The dance proper is not simply the "unexpected passage over, / To make a frightful pleasure, that is all" requested by Vermandero, but the "wild distracted measure, / Though out of form and figure" promised by Alibius. It consists, apparently, of the madmen's morris and the fool's measure (4.3.65-68). A measure is, of course, a partic-ular kind of grave and stately dance, and a morris, though usually a fantastic and occasionally a grotesque dance, is not quite as antic as

Jonson's "preposterous change and gesticulation." It is probable, then, that Alibius' inmates here perform wild and distracted versions of legitimate and recognizable dances. They may have performed a dance of utter disorder and chaos, or they may have danced a true measure and a true morris, but neither of those possibilities is supported by what little textual evidence we have. Lollio does refer to "the whole measure" (68), yet the adjectives "wild and distracted" earlier given the word "measure" may easily be understood here. All the other evidence points toward the likelihood that the measure seen by Alibius and Isabella is a measure indeed, but a travestied one, perhaps like the "mad measure" in *The Lords' Masque*. Alibius had said that he wants a "measure, / Though out of form and figure" (3.3.262-63), and just before the dance he tells Lollio that "the more absurdity" there is in the dance, "The more commends it" (4.3.58-59). After it is done, he shows his satisfaction by judging it "perfect."[14]

It also seems certain that Antonio and Franciscus take part in the dance. There is no reason for them not to; they are, so far as Alibius knows, legitimate inmates. Lollio would not have Antonio practicing his "footmanship" (84-101) just before the dance if the counterfeit fool were not expected to perform. Most convincing, though, is Lollio's advice to Franciscus about how to get rid of Antonio: "Only reserve him till the masque be past, and if you find him not *now in the dance* yourself, I'll show you" (201-02; my emphasis). Lollio does order Franciscus in just after this speech, but this is probably done so that Franciscus can join in the formal entry of all the dancers as ordered by Alibius: "Away then, and guide them in, Lollio" (207).

This dance, then, brings together for the first and last time all the subplot's characters: Isabella watches, Alibius judges, Lollio guides in and presents his corps de ballet, the hospital's legitimate inmates dance their distracted measure and morris, and the counterfeit madman and counterfeit fool join in the dance before Isabella even as they mark each other out for future quarrel. In this dramatic event the Jacobean audience is given an almost emblematic vision of all the plotting and counter-plotting that has gone on in the subplot as well as, by several ratios, the main plot. We see Alibius, who thrives by his madmen and his fools, judging the performance according to the "coin and credit for our pains" (214) it will return. We see the triumvirate of would-be cuckolders—Antonio, Franciscus, and Lollio—each of whom is now thoroughly embroiled in plans to earn Isabella's favors. We see Isabella herself, who has just attempted to meet Antonio in his own guise and been rebuffed:

> No, I have no beauty now,
> Nor never had, but what was in my garments.
> You a quick-sighted lover? Come not near me!
> Keep your caparisons, y'are aptly clad;
> I came a feigner to return stark mad.
>
> (4.3.131-35)

We see her next, after the dance, standing silently by her un-cuckolded husband as he tells Tomazo, the murdered Alonzo's rightly vengeful brother, that Franciscus and Antonio entered his hospital in disguise on the day of the murder.

The dance in *The Changeling* is not just preparation for a wedding entertainment that for some reason never materializes. It is sufficient in itself as a crystallization of actions in the subplot in the same way as the subplot is sufficient in itself as a crystallization of the main plot. The dance is a kind of icon-in-motion of all the distracted foolishness and madness that Lollio manipulates, that Alibius uses as a commodity for himself and as a prision for his wife, that Antonio and Franciscus take refuge in under the very eyes of Alibius, that the changelings use to shield their lust as well as their plots to eliminate each other, that Isabella sees and quite clearly rejects. As many critics have observed, Beatrice sees a more serious version of it in her "bridge of blood" (5.3.81), but she welcomes the feigning. On both Levin's "efficient" and "formal" levels, the masque is no more missing from *The Changeling* than is the marriage between Beatrice and Alonzo it was originally to honor or the marriage between Beatrice and Alsemero it might more appropriately have graced. Marriage and masque are alike eradicated by the revelation that each is inhabited by changelings. Alsemero puts the similarity of kind, and the difference of degree, quite succinctly: "I have two other / That were more close disguis'd than your two could be, / E'er since the deed was done" (5.3.127-29). "Close disguise" is the very essence of the dance: the close disguise of madness or of fooling that harbors threats to the marriage of the two on-stage spectators and even to the life of another so disguised. Close disguise is the very essence of the main plot as well, as Alsemero sees when he submits his list of changes at the play's end (5.3.196-203). William Empson exaggerated only slightly when he wrote that this dance of madmen, fools, and disguised suitors with villainous plots in their heads is "not merely a fine show on the stage but the chief source of the ideas of the play."[15] Both the play and the dance are composed of changes.

Levin does this scene an injustice, I think, when he admits other business in the subplot to his category of "formal" or analogical links between plots but relegates the dance to the category of "efficient" links, casting it as an interlude of promise on the road to a missing scene. In fact, and here we must venture beyond the text, the dramatic effect of this scene may be something closer to what Levin calls "the more complex integrative effect of the 'final' synthesis"[16] of plots.

This dance is the one moment when the emotional unity of the plots, their affective affinity, is most perfectly rendered. Here in a distracted measure and madmen's morris— too mad and distracted for a neatly analogical ratio to apply—are literal madness and natural folly, a choreographer of inmates who works in earnest expectation of carnal reward, two suitors close disguised in plots against each other and in confident hopes of cuckolding one spectator by tumbling with the other, a husband who has looked outside for sexual threats that are inside, and, in the sole negative analogy, a wife whose eyes have just been shown to be sentinels to her judgment. The "changes" reeled off by the characters who survive the action (5.3.196-215) will convey to the audience the affinity between plots, but the dramatic rendering is here, in the actual "changes" of wild distracted dancing. After this, the subplot has done its business in the play. To ask for the "real" masque, the comic deflations, the motive for revealing the pretenders,[17] is to ask a subplot that has primarily formal and final links suddenly to develop its material and efficient ones. Bradbrook observed of The Changeling that "the subplot is connected with the main plot chiefly by implication. It acts as a kind of parallel or reflection in a different mode: their relationship is precisely that of masque and antimasque, say the two halves of Jonson's Masque of Queens."[18] An antimasque is sometimes related materially or causally to its masque, but it usually connects in formal and final ways.

The masque of madmen in *The Duchess of Malfi* is occasionally compared to this wild measure and madmen's morris in *The Changeling*. Farr, for example, calls it an "obvious parallel,"[19] and Cornelia juxtaposes the contrast between madness and the Duchess in Webster's play with the comparison between madness and Beatrice in Middleton and Rowley's.[20] We might add the comparison between the madmen and Ferdinand in *The Duchess of Malfi* and the contrast between madness and Isabella's sanity in *The Changeling*. But these are easily found parallels; the two interludes actually have quite different functions in their respective plays and different effects upon their respective audiences. In *The Duchess of Malfi* the masque is a weapon of revenge that fails to intimidate its intended victim and instead backfires on the revenger. The dance in *The Changeling* is not a revels of revenge. Unlikely though it may at first seem, that dance is not nearly so comparable to the entertainment in *The Duchess of Malfi* as it is to the masque in *The Maid's Tragedy*, which of course also precedes a particularly disastrous wedding night. I have stressed not the very real differences between that nuptial masque and the events to come but the analogy between the ungovernable north wind Boreas and the disorder in the King's two unions (the union of the marriage between Amintor and Evadne and the union of the kingdom). The dance in *The Changeling* plays a comparable role. In this scene, the theater audience sees, writ small, the basic "changes" of the larger tragedy. This is not a new observation. But the observation has depended upon the bare stage direction "The Madmen and Fools dance" when it could be immeasurably strengthened in the same way the dramatic effect in the theater is immeasurably enriched: by drawing attention to those two characters besides the true madmen and the true fools who are dancing, and why; to the character who has choreographed and presented the dance, and to what ends; to what the on-stage spectators see, and what—because of changes close disguised—they fail to see.

Epilogue: Woe and Wonder

Far from disappearing from the stage when James died, the masque virtually invaded tragedy under Charles. The plays of Ford, Massinger, and Shirley, for example, are studded with masques and masque-like elements. But the masque in Caroline tragedy warrants a separate study, for in the 1630s the device begins to shed two characteristics of its Jacobean incarnations. Gone, or at least going, are many of the tightly symbiotic links between inserted masque and encompassing play; gone too are some of the jarring contrasts between the matter or manner of the masque and the matter or manner of the play. This is not to suggest that masques in later Stuart plays are dramatically ineffective compared to their Jacobean forebears; both periods have successful as well as unsuccessful examples in their repertoires. To beat the Caroline inserted masque with a Jacobean stick is to acquiesce in the notion that the later Stuart drama "declines" or becomes "decadent." Theatrical history is not so simple, and the history of the inserted masque—as Ewbank noted—cannot be independently charted.

But what, then, can one conclude about the masque in Jacobean tragedy? Thus far I have argued, for the most part implicitly, against the existence of such an entity: we have not *the* masque in Jacobean tragedy but a number of masques in a number of Jacobean tragedies. This is far more a study of six plays that contain masques than a study of the inserted masque, and as such it is a plea to let seventeenth-century plays that show little interest in categories stand unencumbered by the critical penchant for categorizing. I have argued against classifying this material by forms or functions of masque or play, and I have argued against arranging this material so that a pattern of influence from playwright to playwright or of development from play to play is made to emerge. My concern throughout is less to define a device than to shed light on some plays by examining what uses they make of a device. On the other hand and *pace* Blake, to generalize is not always to be an idiot. Although an inserted masque, like its encompassing play, is always a special instance, the relationship of masque to tragedy remains stable. In every one of these six plays that relationship consists of two components: one celebrating decorum through a show full of wonder and honorable praise, the other violating decorum by exploiting disguise and then subsiding in madness, mayhem, or murder. The two components are not always in the same position with respect to each other. In *Antonio's Revenge, The Revenger's Tragedy, The Maid's Tragedy*, and *Women Beware Women*, decorum inheres (though sometimes only potentially) in the masque itself and indecorum appears in the actions of the play's masquers and spectators. In *The Duchess of Malfi* and *The Changeling* the decorum lies in a spectator's reaction while the masque is madness or folly. Ben Jonson's characters Scriben and Clench defined a masque as show and disguise; I suggested at the outset and I submit again now that these are the two major and sharply warring elements that fix a masque to the tragedy in which it appears. A masque in Jacobean tragedy is both wonder and woe, "tied to rules of flattery" and "treason's licence," show and disguise, masque and mask.

But what is the significance of finding this kind of juxtaposition between decorum and indecorum, order and disorder, in six of the finest tragedies produced in the Jacobean theater? Two other students of the masques in these plays have given special weight to this relationship between masque and play. At the end of his chapter on tragedy, David Laird writes,

> . . . at times the masque represents either an unreal or pretended order which is ironically exposed as in *The Maid's Tragedy* or *Women Beware Women* or an ideal and divinely sanctioned order to which the disorder and violence of the play are contrasted as in *Byron's Tragedy*.

In both *The Duchess of Malfi* and *The Changeling* the masque serves as a grotesque and mocking parody. The relation of the inserted masque to play may be that of masque to antimasque or conversely that of antimasque to masque.[1]

Inga-Stina Ewbank is discussing the same relationship when she concludes her long essay on "these pretty devices" (the phrase is Shirley's):

> Finally, while the inserted masque tends to have a realistic motivation, it also at the same time changes the structure of the scene where it occurs, and of the play as a whole, in a direction away from realism. The masque often gives the playwright an opportunity to introduce ritual and stylized action in a play which ostensibly is steering away from the ritualistic. The masque then becomes a kind of mediator between convention and realism.[2]

Decorum and indecorum, order and disorder, masque and anti-masque, ritual and nonritual, even convention and realism: these are all different labels for the same two terms of the masque-tragedy relationship. But neither Laird nor Ewbank explores that relationship further. Ewbank's rather abrupt ending infuriated Stephen Orgel, who was driven to ask a question that he complains "evidently does not interest Mrs. Ewbank": "But why, at this particular moment in English culture, should playwrights and audiences have begun so intensely to require mediators between convention and realism?"[3] Why indeed? Why in this first quarter of the seventeenth century, and not before or in quite the same way since, do the best dramatists present their audiences with spectacular scenes that throw violently together the orderly decorum inherent in celebratory court entertainment with the disordered indecorum of madness and murder?

There are partial answers to that question in the three historical factors cited earlier: the strong impact of Kyd's play within a play, the special talents of boy companies and the facilities of indoor private theaters, and, undoubtedly most influential, the appearance of lavish masques at the court of King James. But there may be another answer too, one that may actually be more helpful in placing this device in its larger context. The impulse that led to the masque in Jacobean tragedy is, I suggest, the same impulse that led the finest minds of the age to dwell almost obsessively on the simultaneously similar and dissimilar nature of things. This impulse is sometimes referred to as the Jacobean sensibility—a useful phrase were it not for the dangers of the definite article. Regardless of label, this impulse is seen in that "universall Monarchy of wit" to which Carew gave Donne title. It is seen in the metaphysical conceit, in which (as Samuel Johnson's still apt definition has it) "the most heterogeneous ideas are yoked by violence together." It is seen in the affection for certain kinds of ambiguity, a predilection that Rosalie Colie has called "paradoxica epidemica."[4] T. S. Eliot called it "a mechanism of sensibility which could devour any kind of experience."[5] In "Whispers of Immortality" (1919), Eliot followed two stanzas on John Webster with this passage:

> Donne, I suppose, was such another
> Who found no substitute for sense,
> To seize and clutch and penetrate;
> Expert beyond experience.

This mechanism, brazenly coaxing elements from divided and distinguished worlds into a single composition, was extremely active in Jacobean England. When it goes to work in poetry, as when Donne writes a line like "Nor ever chaste, except you ravish me" or a poem like "A Valediction: Forbidding Mourning," we tend to call it affecting the metaphysics. When it appears at court, as when Faith, Hope, and Charity must leave the defiled (and unhappily named) King Christian IV to sit sick and spewing in the lower hall, we sometimes speak of mannerism.[6] In the theater it may take many forms, such as the contrapuntal juxtaposition of main plot and subplot in *The Changeling*. The same mechanism is at work when Antonio and Vindice turn revels to revenge, when Evadne turns nuptial triumph to travesty, when the masque of madmen leaves the Duchess of Malfi Duchess still, when the Duke in *Women Beware Women* watches "great mischiefs / Mask in expected pleasures," and when, in *The Changeling*, a nuptial dance intended to please a lady whose beauty has changed to ugly whoredom is performed by one who has changed from a little ass to a great fool and another who has changed from a little wit to be stark mad (5.3.197-208). "For contraries," wrote Sir Thomas Browne in a different context a decade after the death of James, "though they destroy one another, are yet the life of one another."[7]

The single most characteristic feature of the masque in Jacobean tragedy is this stark contrariety in the way the inherent splendor of masquery gives sudden way to particularly awesome acts of violence or, conversely, in the way droll or grotesque bits of antic masquery contrast with high tragic seriousness elsewhere in the action. Whatever individual work the masque may do in an individual play is done by means of those contrasts, those tensions. The more general contribution of this device to Jacobean tragedy, beyond its many particular contributions to particular plays, comes from its ability to create swiftly and richly, by a form of dramatic shorthand no longer available to the stage, just such tensions between that which is full of wonder and that which is full of woe. The Cardinal's reaction to the masque in *Women Beware Women* (5.2.198-200) might therefore be pressed into service as a more general epigraph:

> The greatest sorrow and astonishment
> That ever struck the general peace of Florence
> Dwells in this hour.

Notes

Introduction

1. *A Tale of a Tub*, ed. C.H. Herford and Percy Simpson, in *Ben Jonson*, III (Oxford: Clarendon, 1927), 5.2.29-31.
2. I have found only five: Inga-Stina Ekeblad [Ewbank], "The 'Impure Art' of John Webster," *RES*, NS 9 (1958), 253-67; Michael Neill, "'The Simetry, Which Gives a Poem Grace': Masque, Imagery, and the Fancy of *The Maid's Tragedy*," *RenD*, NS 3 (1970), 111-35; Glynne Wickham, "Masque and Anti-masque in *The Tempest*," *E&S*, 28 (1975), 1-14; John D. Cox, "*Henry VIII* and the Masque," *ELH*, 45 (1978), 390-409; and Donald K. Hedrick, "The Masquing Principle in Marston's *The Malcontent*," *ELR*, 8 (1978), 24-42. The first two will be discussed in the sections on *The Duchess of Malfi* and *The Maid's Tragedy*.
3. Inga-Stina Ewbank, "'These Pretty Devices': A Study of Masques in Plays," in *A Book of Masques in Honour of Allardyce Nicoll*, ed. T.J.B. Spencer, et al. (Cambridge: Cambridge Univ. Press, 1967), p. 409.
4. M. Bonaventure Cornelia used a similar principle in "The Function of the Masque in Jacobean Tragedy and Tragicomedy," Diss. Fordham 1968. She writes, "most often what the dramatist himself has designated a masque has been accepted as such" (p. 2).
5. All of these plays are, to a greater or lesser extent, tragedies of revenge. In discussing them I draw upon the standard critical literature, as my notes and bibliography indicate. As the present volume went to press, a new and very thorough study appeared: Charles A. Hallett and Elaine S. Hallett, *The Revenger's Madness: A Study of Revenge Tragedy Motifs* (Lincoln: Univ. of Nebraska Press, 1980). The Halletts examine six motifs—the ghost, madness, the delay, the play-within-the-

play, multiple murders, and the death of the avenger—in *The Spanish Tragedy, Antonio's Revenge, Hamlet,* and *The Revenger's Tragedy.* I regret that publication deadlines prevent my incorporating into my comments some of their significant insights; I regret also their lack of sufficient differentiation between plays-within-plays and masques-within-plays.

6. Unless otherwise noted, the dates assigned to these plays are those given in Alfred Harbage, *Annals of English Drama 975–1700,* rev. S. Schoenbaum (London: Methuen, 1964); hereafter cited as *Annals.*

Chapter 1—The Critical Heritage

1. *The Elizabethan Dumb Show: The History of a Dramatic Convention* (Cambridge, Mass.: Harvard Univ. Press, 1966).
2. *Les Masques anglais: Etude sur les ballets et la vie de cour en Angleterre, 1512–1640* (1909; rpt. New York: Benjamin Blom, 1964), pp. 497-98.
3. *The Relations of Shirley's Plays to the Elizabethan Drama* (New York: Columbia Univ. Press, 1914), pp. 79-80.
4. *The Elizabethan Stage* (Oxford: Clarendon, 1923), I, 186-90.
5. Chambers, I, 188, 189.
6. Chambers, I, 190.
7. *The Court Masque: A Study in the Relationship between Poetry and the Revels* (Cambridge: Cambridge Univ. Press, 1927). On masques and masque elements in plays, see pp. 276-301.
8. Welsford, p. 294.
9. Welsford, p. 292.
10. "The Play Within the Play," in *A Series of Papers on Shakespeare and the Theatre* (London: Shakespeare Assn., 1927), pp. 134-56.
11. Boas, p. 155.
12. "The Inserted Masque in Elizabethan and Jacobean Drama," Diss. Wisconsin 1955.
13. Laird, pp. 140-41.
14. Laird, p. 173.
15. "The Play Within a Play: An Elizabethan Dramatic Device," *E&S*, NS 13 (1960), 36-48.
16. Brown, pp. 43, 40.
17. "Zur Entwicklung des 'Play Within a Play' im elisabethanischen Drama," *SJH*, 97 (1961), 134-52.
18. "Forms and Functions of the Play Within a Play," *RenD*, 8 (1965), 41-61.
19. Mehl, "Forms and Functions," pp. 42, 43.
20. Mehl, "Forms and Functions," p. 60.
21. Mehl, "Forms and Functions," p. 61.
22. Inga-Stina Ewbank, " 'These Pretty Devices': A Study of Masques in Plays," in *A Book of Masques in Honour of Allardyce Nicoll,* ed. T.J.B. Spencer, et al. (Cambridge: Cambridge Univ. Press, 1967), pp. 405-48.

23. Ewbank, p. 409.
24. Ewbank, p. 411n.
25. Ewbank, p. 412.
26. Ewbank, p. 443.
27. "Antimasque," *EIC*, 18 (1968), p. 319. Author's emphasis.
28. Ewbank, p. 447.
29. Ewbank, pp. 447-48
30. Ewbank, p. 448.
31. "The Dramatic Function of the Masque in English Drama, 1592–1642," Diss. Texas 1967.
32. Shaw, p. 351.
33. M. Bonaventure Cornelia, S.S.J., "The Function of the Masque in Jacobean Tragedy and Tragicomedy," Diss. Fordham 1968.
34. These categories are Cornelia's chapter headings.
35. "The Fatal Masque: A Study of Visual Metaphor and Dramatic Convention in Renaissance Tragedy," Diss. Princeton 1969.
36. Fishman, p. 197.
37. "Variations in the Use of the Masque in English Revenge Tragedy," *YES*, 3 (1973), 44-54.
38. Golding, p. 44. There is evidence that Golding has read Ewbank, but he has apparently not found Laird, Cornelia, or Fishman. He does cite Shaw but adds "I have not been able to consult this work" (p. 44n).
39. Golding, p. 48.
40. Golding, p. 48.
41. *Metatheatre: A New View of Dramatic Form* (New York: Hill and Wang, 1963).
42. James L. Calderwood, *Shakespearean Metadrama: The Argument of the Play in "Titus Andronicus," "Love's Labor's Lost," "Romeo and Juliet," "A Midsummer Night's Dream," and "Richard II"* (Minneapolis: Univ. of Minnesota Press, 1971), p. 5.
43. "Deadly Sins of Criticism, or, Seven Ways to Get Shakespeare Wrong," *SQ*, 9 (1958), p. 305.
44. By, respectively, Robert J. Nelson (New Haven: Yale Univ. Press, 1958) and Robert Egan (New York: Columbia Univ. Press, 1975).
45. Lillian Wilds, *Shakespeare's Character-Dramatists: A Study of a Character Type in Shakespearean Tragedy through Hamlet*, Salzburg Studies in English Literature: Elizabethan and Renaissance Studies, 46 (Salzburg: Institut für englische Sprache und Literatur, 1975), p. 218.

Chapter 2—Kyd's Play, James's Masque, and London Theaters

1. There is a good summary of the stage history in Philip Edwards, Introd., *The Spanish Tragedy*, by Thomas Kyd, Revels (London: Methuen, 1959), pp. lxvi-lxviii. Edwards notes that "references to and parodies of the play are innumerable in the earlier seventeenth century, but their existence does not depend upon a live theatrical tradition; but the successive editions of 1610, 1615, 1618, 1623, and 1633 seem

to speak of more than a literary interest" (p. lxvii). Quotations from *The Spanish Tragedy* are taken from Edwards' edition.

2. Those who do write on the internal drama in relation to the frame often end by turning Kyd into a Pirandellian metadramatist whose main purpose is to examine the nature of reality and illusion. See, for examples of this tendency, Anne Righter, *Shakespeare and the Idea of the Play* (Baltimore: Penguin, 1962), pp. 70-74; Leslie A. Fiedler, "The Defense of the Illusion and the Creation of Myth," *English Institute Essays*, ed. D.A. Robertson, Jr. (New York: Columbia Univ. Press, 1949), pp. 74-94; and, for the most sober assessment, Harriet Hawkins, "Fabulous Counterfeits: Dramatic Construction and Dramatic Perspective in *The Spanish Tragedy*, *A Midsummer Night's Dream*, and *The Tempest*," *ShakS*, 6 (1970), 51-65.

3. Hawkins, p. 56.

4. Although there are persons "above" in many scenes, it is possible that Andrea and Revenge are also on an upper level.

5. *Elizabethan Revenge Tragedy 1587–1642* (Princeton: Princeton Univ. Press, 1940), p. 71.

6. Edwards, p. 8n.

7. Edwards, p. 8n.

8. There is a cogent analysis of this speech in David Laird, "Hieronimo's Dilemma," *SP*, 62 (1965), 137-46. Laird concentrates on the first twenty lines (and is a good antidote to Bowers on that passage), whereas I am interested in what comes after the conclusion in line 20.

9. See Ronald Broude, "Human and Divine Vengeance in the Tragedy of Revenge," Diss. Columbia 1967, and "Revenge and Revenge Tragedy in Renaissance England," *RenQ*, 28 (1975), 38-58.

10. Bowers, p. 71.

11. On "applies our drift," see Edwards, p. 101n.

12. I am trusting both the stage direction and Hieronimo's explicit orders. See S.F. Johnson, "*The Spanish Tragedy*, or Babylon Revisited," in *Essays on Shakespeare and Elizabethan Drama in Honor of Hardin Craig*, ed. Richard Hosley (Columbia: Univ. of Missouri Press, 1962), pp. 23-36.

13. This is the prophecy of Tecnicus in John Ford, *The Broken Heart*, in *The Anchor Anthology of Jacobean Drama*, II, ed. Richard C. Harrier (Garden City: Anchor, 1963), 5.2.147.

14. Stephen Orgel and Roy C. Strong, *Inigo Jones: The Theatre of the Stuart Court* (London: Sotheby-Parke Bernet, 1973), I, 79.

15. Inga-Stina Ewbank, " 'The Eloquence of Masques': A Retrospective View of Masque Criticism," *RenD*, NS 1 (1968), p. 326.

16. Dolora Cunningham, "The Jonsonian Masque as a Literary Form," *ELH*, 22 (1955), 108-24; rpt. in *Ben Jonson: A Collection of Critical Essays*, ed. Jonas A. Barish (Englewood Cliffs: Prentice-Hall, 1963), p. 173.

17. On the Jonsonian masque in its political context, the standard study is still Mary Sullivan, *Court Masques of James I* (New York: Putnam, 1913).

18. Glynne Wickham, "The Stuart Mask," in his *Shakespeare's Dramatic Heritage: Collected Studies in Mediaeval, Tudor and Shakespearean Drama* (New York: Barnes and Noble, 1969), p. 116.

19. Francis Bacon, "Of Masques and Triumphs," in *Francis Bacon: A Selection of His Works*, ed. Sidney Warhaft (New York: Odyssey, 1965), p. 145.

20. *Hymenaei*, in *Ben Jonson: The Complete Masques*, ed. Stephen Orgel (New Haven: Yale Univ. Press, 1969), ll. 1-25. All quotations from Jonson's masques are taken from this edition.

21. Stephen Orgel, Introd., *Ben Jonson: The Complete Masques*, p. 5. Orgel adds that "the single, obviously anomalous, exception is *The Gypsies Metamorphosed*, which caters to Buckingham's histrionic talents" (p. 5n).

22. Orgel, Introd., p. 1.

23. "Image, Form, and Theme in *A Mask*," in her *Images and Themes in Five Poems by Milton* (Cambridge: Harvard Univ. Press, 1957), pp. 112-61; rpt. in *A Maske at Ludlow: Essays on Milton's* Comus, ed. John S. Diekhoff (Cleveland: Case Western Reserve Univ. Press, 1968), pp. 129-30. Tuve is thinking primarily of *Comus*, but her words apply to many other masques as well.

24. "Jacobean Tragedy and the Mannerist Style," *ShS*, 26 (1973), p. 57.

25. As quoted in Chambers, I, 172n. Cf. Dudley Carleton's account of *Blackness* as quoted in Herford and Simpson, X, 449: "and in the cuming owt, a banquet which was prepared for the king in the great chamber was overturned table and all before it was skarce touched. It were infinit to tell you what losses there were of chaynes, Jewels, purces, and such like loose ware. And one woeman amongst the rest lost her honesty, for which she was caried to the porters lodge being surprised at her busines on the top of the Taras."

26. See D.J. Gordon, "Poet and Architect: The Intellectual Setting of the Quarrel Between Ben Jonson and Inigo Jones," *JWCI*, 12 (1949), 152-78.

27. John W. Cunliffe, "The Masque in Shakespeare's Plays," *Archiv*, 125 (1910), p. 76.

28. Chambers, I, 149.

29. "The Poetics of Spectacle," *NLH*, 2 (1971), p. 367.

30. Wickham, "The Stuart Mask," p. 104.

31. Andrew J. Sabol, *Songs and Dances for the Stuart Masque* (Providence: Brown Univ. Press, 1959), p. 1. See also his edition of *Four Hundred Songs and Dances from the Stuart Masque* (Providence: Brown Univ. Press, 1978).

32. Sabol, p. 1. The emphasis in Sabol's outline is obviously choreographic rather than literary, but so, in the main, is the emphasis in masques within plays. For the literary perspective, see Cunningham, and Stephen Orgel, *The Jonsonian Masque* (Cambridge, Mass.: Harvard Univ. Press, 1967).

33. Sabol, p. 7.

34. Tuve, p. 131n.

35. *Annals.* Marston's is sometimes called *The Huntingdon Masque.*
36. Repertories for all the children's troupes, with dates of first performance, are given in Michael Shapiro, *Children of the Revels: The Boy Companies of Shakespeare's Time and Their Plays* (New York: Columbia Univ. Press, 1977), pp. 261-68. The dates I give are those of Shapiro's lists, not the *Annals.*
37. Shapiro, pp. 235-36.
38. John Marston, *Antonio and Mellida*, ed. G.K. Hunter, Regents (Lincoln: Univ. of Nebraska Press, 1965), 5.2. All quotations from this play come from this edition.
39. *The Malcontent*, ed. Bernard Harris, New Mermaids (London: Benn, 1967), Induction, 75, 80-81. All quotations from *The Malcontent* are taken from this edition.
40. Marston's and Middleton's masques have been cited; Chapman's *The Masque of the Middle Temple and Lincoln's Inn* was performed at court in 1613.
41. As quoted in Thomas Marc Parrott, ed., *The Plays and Poems of George Chapman*, I (London: Routledge, 1910), p. 591. Quotations from *The Tragedy of Byron* are from this edition.
42. Laird sees this masque as a comment on Byron as well as on the King's two women (p. 126), and Cornelia writes that "it can be seen as a commentary on the play as a whole, at the center of whose action is Henry's desire and attempt to win back Byron's loyalty and reconcile the general to himself" (p. 127). I am not convinced. The relations between the masque and the Byron-Henry conflict are too general (like rivers with "salmons in poth," Fluellen might say). There is no reason not to take Henry's word that the masque pertains to a quarrel between his Queen and his mistress, especially when we have evidence that there was such a quarrel in the original play. In *The Tragedy of Byron* as we now have it, the masque is little more than an excrescence.
43. This summary leans on the excellent short discussion in Andrew Gurr, *The Shakespearean Stage 1574–1642* (Cambridge: Cambridge Univ. Press, 1970), pp. 82-111 and especially pp. 82-83. Gurr's book is, in turn, a summary of the material in Chambers; G.E. Bentley, *The Jacobean and Caroline Stage*, 7 vols. (Oxford: Clarendon, 1941-68); and other standard reference works.
44. Shapiro, p. 68. The very rigid distinctions between the public theater audience and the private theater coterie urged in Alfred Harbage, *Shakespeare and the Rival Traditions* (New York: Macmillan, 1952) are, as Shapiro implies, no longer widely accepted.
45. Shaw, p. 231.
46. Throughout, for example, Laird, Shaw, Cornelia, and Fishman.

Chapter 3—Marston's *Antonio's Revenge*

1. Each title page says that the play is given "as it hath beene sundry times acted, by the children of Paules."

2. 1599–1601. Dating these two plays with precision is all but impossible. They cannot have been first performed before the Children of Paul's resumed acting in 1599 or after the plays were entered in the Stationers' Register in October of 1601. Determining the chronological relationship of *Antonio's Revenge* to *Hamlet* is especially difficult, and we shall probably never know with certainty whether Shakespeare's play preceded or followed Marston's, or whether both are dependent upon the *Ur-Hamlet*. There are summaries of the evidence in Hunter, Introd., *Antonio's Revenge*, pp. xviii-xxi, in Gair, Introd., *Antonio's Revenge*, pp. 12-19, and in Philip J. Finkelpearl, *John Marston of the Middle Temple* (Cambridge, Mass.: Harvard Univ. Press, 1969), pp. 268-71. The present discussion refrains from taking sides since analogies noticed here between *Antonio's Revenge* and *Hamlet* do not depend upon a theory of priority.

3. Hunter, Introd., *Antonio's Revenge*, p. x. See also his *"Henry IV* and the Elizabethan Two-Part Play," *RES*, NS 5 (1954), 236-48.

4. The actor who played Feliche in *Antonio and Mellida* may have played Pandulpho in *Antonio's Revenge* (Hunter, Introd., *Antonio and Mellida*, p. 9n).

5. See *OED, sb*, 6 and 7.

6. Here Marston's Piero foreshadows the choleric King James, who is reported to have shouted to the weary masquers in Jonson's *Pleasure Reconciled to Virtue* (1618), "What did you make me come here for? Devil take you all, dance" (Bentley, IV, 671).

7. There is no real motivation for Piero's acts in *Antonio and Mellida* except the vague "Pish! I prosecute my family's revenge" (1.1.87). For an audience which did not demand motivation from its villains, Marston did not need to elaborate in *Antonio's Revenge*—unless he was underlining the justice of Antonio's vengeance by comparison to the speciousness of Piero's.

8. Biblical quotations are from *The Geneva Bible: A Facsimile of the 1560 Edition*, Introd. by Lloyd E. Berry (Madison: Univ. of Wisconsin Press, 1969). On the importance of the villain's being hoist with his own petard, see Broude, "Revenge and Revenge Tragedy in Renaissance England," pp. 54-55.

9. *"Venit in nostras manus / Tandem vindicta, venit et tota quidem."* Gair quotes Keltie's translation: "At length has vengeance come into my power, and that to the full." The words are those spoken by Atreus when he sees Thyestes snared at last.

10. See Ronald Broude, *"Vindicta Filia Temporis*: Three English Forerunners of the Elizabethan Revenge Play," *JEGP*, 72 (1973), 489-502 and esp. p. 500. See also his "Revenge and Revenge Tragedy in Renaissance England," pp. 53-54.

11. Finkelpearl, pp. 154, 158.

12. On all three dumb shows, see Mehl, *The Elizabethan Dumb Show*, pp. 125-32. Mehl concludes that the third pantomine "shows in a short and unambiguous scene how Piero is threatened and hated from all sides,

thus preparing the way for the last act which contains the traditional masque of revengers and the bloody end" (p. 131). While this is basically accurate, Mehl neglects the significance of Galeatzo's reading a paper to the two Senators. And it is difficult to see how the masque of revengers can be "traditional" when Marston's is the first play in English drama to use it.

13. This is another way in which Strotzo resembles Pedringano. The second witness in Kyd's play is the letter from Pedringano to Lorenzo that is intercepted by Hieronimo (3.7.32-39). On the importance of the Mosaic code to *The Spanish Tragedy*, see Johnson, pp. 29-30. Also cf. Matthew 18:15-16.

14. Some members of Marston's audience might see this need for additional proof as another reason for Antonio to have refrained from stabbing Piero earlier (3.2.87-91).

15. Finkelpearl, p. 158.

16. Broude, "*Vindicta Filia Temporis*," p. 501.

17. On the choice and feats of Hercules in English Renaissance drama, see Eugene M. Waith, *The Herculean Hero in Marlowe, Chapman, Shakespeare and Dryden* (New York: Columbia Univ. Press, 1962). Though he does not mention Marston, Waith probably would admit Antonio to the company of his other Herculean heroes.

18. Views representative of the first camp are Golding's suggestion that "what perhaps contributes towards the condemnation of Antonio is the use of a masque to effect his revenge" (p. 48), and the idea that Marston is parodying the Kydian revenger argued in P.J. Ayres, "Marston's *Antonio's Revenge*: The Morality of the Revenging Hero," *SEL*, 12 (1972), 359-74. More or less in the second camp are Ewbank in " 'These Pretty Devices' " (p. 443), Shaw (pp. 272-77), and Finkelpearl (pp. 150-61).

19. E.g., Mehl, "Forms and Functions," p. 47.

20. Fishman, p. 95.

21. Brown, p. 43.

22. *Dances of England and France from 1450 to 1600* (London: Routledge and Kegan Paul, 1949), pp. 52-53. Arnold Dolmetsch's setting for keyboard of the 1570 lute book's measure is on pp. 53-54. See also Sabol, *passim*.

23. See David G. O'Neill, "The Influence of Music in the Works of John Marston," *M&L*, 53 (1972), 122-33, 293-308, 400-10. There is a good summary of the state of our knowledge in Shapiro, pp. 233-55.

24. Dometsch, p. 1.

25. See esp. Ayres' article cited above (note 18).

Chapter 4—Tourneur's *The Revenger's Tragedy*

1. Whether Cyril Tourneur was indeed the author of *The Revenger's Tragedy* is still the subject of debate, but by general agreement, the play is usually ascribed to him. For a concise summary of the arguments for Tourneur and for Middleton (the only other likely candidate), see

Foakes, Introd., *The Revenger's Tragedy*, pp. xlviii-liv. On the basis of the evidence, and for convenience's sake, I shall consider the play Tourneur's.

2. On Tourneur's play see esp. pp. 132-38.
3. Bowers, p. 134.
4. Bowers, p. 132.
5. Bowers, p. 134.
6. Bowers, p. 137.
7. See 2.2.124-29; 3.1.13-15, 26; 3.6.23; 5.1.115-17, 175-85. Bowers himself refers to "the strife among the duke's ambitious sons" (p. 137).
8. Shaw, pp. 291-300.
9. Shaw, p. 269.
10. Shaw, p. 295.
11. Shaw, p. 292. Here Shaw gives the speech incorrectly to Spurio; she correctly assigns it to Supervacuo on p. 297. Allardyce Nicoll, in his edition of *The Works of Cyril Tourneur* (1930; rpt. New York: Russell and Russell, 1963), reversed the headings of the last four speeches of this scene (5.1), giving Ambitioso's lines to Supervacuo and vice versa. Recent editors have rejected Nicoll's arguments for this change and returned to the quarto's speech headings. See Foakes, pp. 119 (collation), 124n.
12. Shaw, p. 298.
13. Shaw, p. 300.
14. Golding, p. 49.
15. Golding, p. 50. Although Golding quotes from Foakes's edition, which follows the quarto in giving the couplet to Supervacuo, he twice refers to the masque as Ambitioso's.
16. L. G. Salingar, "*The Revenger's Tragedy* and the Morality Tradition," *Scrutiny*, 6 (1938), p. 402.
17. See, for example, Morris Palmer Tilley, *A Dictionary of the Proverbs in England in the Sixteenth and Seventeenth Centuries* (Ann Arbor: Univ. of Michigan Press, 1950), K90.
18. Thomas Sackville and Thomas Norton, *Gorboduc, or Ferrex and Porrex*, ed. Irby B. Cauthen, Jr., Regents (Lincoln: Univ. of Nebraska Press, 1970), 2.1.143. Other quotations from *Gorboduc* are taken from this edition.
19. Foakes glosses "marrow" as "figuratively, delicious food for his revenge" (p. 126n).
20. This term is defined by Francis Berry in *The Shakespeare Inset: Word and Picture* (London: Routledge and Kegan Paul, 1965), p. 12. It is "likely to occur in the opening or second scene of the first act . . . (though it *may* occur later) . . . : it informs the audience of what they need to know before they can follow what is to be shown."
21. Leslie Sanders, "*The Revenger's Tragedy*: A Play on the Revenge Play," *Ren&R*, 10 (1974), p. 27.
22. "Light cares speak; greater ones are silent (*Hippolytus*, 607). Seneca has *ingentes* (huge) where Hippolito quotes *maiores*.
23. Cf. the similar rhetorical climax in Vindice's "This night, this hour—/

This minute, now—" (2.2.160-61).

24. Vindice's reference to nine years is surely also a rhetorical flourish. Cf. his "Nine coaches waiting" (2.1.206) ánd Othello's "I would have him nine years a-killing!" (*Oth.*, 4.1.175). The bastard Edmund in *King Lear* "hath been out nine years" (*Lr.*, 1.1.31) and Isabella's mother in *Women Beware Women* has been dead for nine years (2.1.104; cf. 3.3.233). One of Ophelia's grave-diggers tells Hamlet that a corpse "will last you some eight year or nine year" before it rots (*Ham.*, 5.1.153-56). Like the more common "seven years," "nine years" served as a synonym for "for a long period." See Tilley, Y25.

25. That this dumb show is particularly appropriate in a play replete with masques and references to revels is argued by Mehl in *The Elizabethan Dumb Show*, pp. 132-33.

26. The text presents a problem here. The quarto gives the speech heading *Spu.* for the line "Then I proclaim myself; now I am duke" (53), but, as editors have observed, a bastard cannot make such an assertion. Allardyce Nicoll lets the heading stand, but he suggests that the line should be Ambitioso's in accordance with claims made at 3.1.13 and 3.6.19 and with Nicoll's own alterations of the headings of 5.1.175-85 (see my note 11 above). Foakes argues forcefully that "the obvious correction, of what looks to be a compositor's misreading, is to alter *Spu* to *Super*" (p. 124n). The same correction is made in the editions of Richard Harrier (*The Anchor Anthology of Jacobean Drama*, II), Lawrence J. Ross (Lincoln: Univ. of Nebraska Press, 1966), and Brian Gibbons (London: Benn, 1967).

27. Cf. Hieronimo's last words: "Pleas'd with their deaths, and eas'd with their revenge, / First take my tongue, and afterwards my heart" (4.4.190-91).

Chapter 5—Beaumont and Fletcher's *The Maid's Tragedy*

1. As quoted by Chambers, IV, 45.

2. Turner, Textual Introd., *The Maid's Tragedy*, p. 3. So also Chambers, III, 224; Howard B. Norland, Introd., *The Maid's Tragedy*, Regents (Lincoln: Univ. of Nebraska Press, 1968), p. xi note; Andrew Gurr, Critical Introd., *The Maid's Tragedy*, Fountainwell (Berkeley: Univ. of California Press, 1969), p. 1.

3. As quoted by Chambers, III, 224.

4: Hosley, in Barroll, et al., p. 134n.

5. Chambers, III, 224; IV, 180.

6. So, for example, Charles M. Gayley, *Beaumont the Dramatist* (New York: Century, 1914), pp. 349-53; E.H.C. Oliphant, *The Plays of Beaumont and Fletcher* (New Haven: Yale Univ. Press, 1927), pp. 182-83; Cyrus Hoy, "The Shares of Fletcher and His Collaborators in the Beaumont and Fletcher Canon," *SB*, 11 (1958), p. 94; Norland, p. xiii; and Turner, p. 3. Fletcher's four scenes are 2.2, 4.1, 5.1, and 5.2.

7. My discussion of the textual history of the play relies on the introduc-

tions of Norland (pp. xxii-xxviii), Gurr (pp. 9-13), and especially Turner (pp. 3-27).

8. Turner, p. 11. Cf. John P. Cutts, *La Musique de Scène de la Troupe de Shakespeare* (Paris: Centre National de la Recherche Scientifique, 1959), p. xv note.

9. Norland, p. xxvii. Norland is following the principles of W.W. Greg, "The Rationale of Copy-Text," *SB*, 3 (1950–51), 19-36.

10. Norland, p. xxvii.

11. Norland, p. xxv.

12. Norland, p. xxv.

13. Gurr, "A Note on the Text," *The Maid's Tragedy*, p. 10.

14. "A Textual Study of Beaumont and Fletcher's *The Maid's Tragedy*," 2 vols., Diss. Virginia 1958; "The Relationship of *The Maid's Tragedy* Q1 and Q2," *PBSA*, 51 (1957), 322-27; "The Printing of Beaumont and Fletcher's *The Maid's Tragedy* Q1 (1619)," *SB*, 13 (1960), 199-220.

15. Turner, Textual Introd., p. 24.

16. Turner, Textual Introd., pp. 10-11.

17. Turner, Textual Introd., p. 11.

18. The same conclusion is reached by Suzanne Gossett, "The Term 'Masque' in Shakespeare and Fletcher, and *The Coxcomb*," *SEL*, 14 (1974), 285-95. Gossett goes beyond textual evidence: "It is unlikely that . . . a masque would have been excised to improve a long play. In this period the masque invaded the drama; the public could not seem to get enough of it" (p. 286).

19. Reyher, p. 315.

20. Ewbank, " 'These Pretty Devices,' " p. 418.

21. Shaw, pp. 227, 231.

22. *Beaumont and Fletcher: A Critical Study* (London: George Allen and Unwin, 1956), p. 35.

23. *Themes and Conventions of Elizabethan Tragedy* (Cambridge: Cambridge Univ. Press, 1935), p. 46.

24. *The John Fletcher Plays* (Cambridge, Mass.: Harvard Univ. Press, 1962), p. 122.

25. "Masque Influence on the Dramaturgy of Beaumont and Fletcher," *MP*, 69 (1971–72), p. 203.

26. Neill, p. 120.

27. Neill, p. 126.

28. Neill, pp. 132-34. Cf. Gossett, "Masque Influence," p. 203.

29. Bradbrook, p. 47.

30. Jean Fuzier, in "La Tragédie de Vengeance Elisabethaine et le Théâtre dans le Théâtre," *RSH*, 145 (1972), 17-33, suggests that the Cynthia-Endymion relationship parallels the Evadne-Amintor one, but he does not explain how the analogy works.

31. Orgel, in *Ben Jonson: The Complete Masques*, pp. 63n, 474. Cf. *Beauty*, 51-55.

32. Jonson's note on his sources is reproduced in *Ben Jonson: The Complete Masques*, p. 511.

33. Hoy, "Jacobean Tragedy and the Mannerist Style," p. 57.
34. D.J. Gordon, "*Hymenaei*: Ben Jonson's Masque of Union," *JWCI*, 8 (1945), see p. 110. On the rebellion of the humors and affections, see pp. 110-18.

Chapter 6—Webster's *The Duchess of Malfi*

1. *Specimens of the English Dramatic Poets Who Lived about the Time of Shakespeare* (1808); rpt. in *John Webster: A Critical Anthology*, ed. G.K. Hunter and S.K. Hunter (Baltimore: Penguin, 1969), p. 57.
2. "The 'Impure Art' of John Webster," in Hunter and Hunter, pp. 206-11.
3. But cf. the edition of Elizabeth M. Brennan, New Mermaid (New York: Hill and Wang, 1965), where the quarto's "masque" is retained (2.3.75) and glossed as a verb meaning "take part in a masque" (p. 34n).
4. See John Russell Brown's note on the way Ferdinand's sexual vocabulary links the common courtesans with the madfolk (p. 115n).
5. Cf. Webster's slightly earlier *The White Devil*, ed. John Russell Brown, Revels (Cambridge, Mass.: Harvard Univ. Press, 1960), where Lodovico enters disguised to kill Vittoria and Flamineo, saying "we have brought you a masque" (5.6.169; the quarto's spelling is 'Maske'). But there is no masque; the line is metaphorical. There is one other occurrence of the word in *The Duchess of Malfi*, in the Third Madman's curse on "the caroche, that brought home my wife from the masque, at three o'clock in the morning! it had a large featherbed in it" (4.2.104-06). Here again there can be no question about the proper modern spelling, and here again the association between masque and lust is clear.
6. F.L. Lucas, Introd., *The Duchess of Malfi*, rev. ed. (New York: Macmillan, 1959), p. 25.
7. Brown, Introd., *Duchess*, p. xxxvi.
8. Lucas, pp. 25-27.
9. By, for example, Shaw (p. 263), and more recently Roger Stilling, *Love and Death in Renaissance Tragedy* (Baton Rouge: Louisiana State Univ. Press, 1976), who writes about Ekeblad's "brilliant piece of scholarly spadework" (p. 243).
10. Ekeblad, pp. 213-14.
11. Ekeblad, p. 214.
12. Brown, Introd., *Duchess*, p. xxxvi note. See also Gunnar Boklund, *The Duchess of Malfi: Sources, Themes, Characters* (Cambridge, Mass.: Harvard Univ. Press, 1962), pp. 110-12, 182.
13. Ekeblad, pp. 208-09. Campion's masque is in *A Book of Masques*.
14. *John Webster's Borrowing* (Berkeley: Univ. of California Press, 1960).
15. Brown gives the setting for this song in Appendix II, pp. 210-13.
16. Brown says "i.e., 'compared to thee'" (p. 79n). I do not think the "compared" is essential (though it may be possible), since the line makes sense without it.
17. "The Eight Madmen in *The Duchess of Malfi*," *SEL*, 7 (1967), p. 345.
18. Brown, p. 120n.

19. *"The Duchess of Malfi," Nineteenth Century,* 87 (1920), 126-32; rpt. in *Twentieth-Century Interpretations of "The Duchess of Malfi": A Collection of Critical Essays,* ed. Norman Rabkin (Englewood Cliffs: Prentice-Hall, 1968), p. 18.
20. Ekeblad, pp. 214-18. Cf. Boklund, p. 112, and Brown, Introd., pp. xxxvi-xxxvii.
21. Boklund, p. 111.
22. Welsford, p. 295. Flamineo is in *The White Devil.*
23. "Madmen as Vaudeville Performers on the Elizabethan Stage," *JEGP,* 30 (1931), pp. 51-52.
24. Robert Rentoul Reed, Jr., *Bedlam on the Jacobean Stage* (Cambridge, Mass.: Harvard Univ. Press, 1952), p. 45.
25. Ekeblad, p. 208.
26. Ekeblad, p. 213n.

Chapter 7—Middleton's *Women Beware Women*

1. Stilling, p. 264.
2. R.B. Parker, "Middleton's Experiments with Comedy and Judgement," in *Jacobean Theatre,* ed. John Russell Brown and Bernard Harris, Stratford-upon-Avon Studies I (1960; rpt. New York: Capricorn, 1967), p. 198.
3. Arthur Brown, p. 40.
4. Samuel Schoenbaum, *Middleton's Tragedies: A Critical Study* (New York: Columbia Univ. Press, 1955), p. 131.
5. Fishman, p. 174. Fishman actually is arguing against the "cantilevered portico" school and in favor of the masque's organic connection with the play. He sees the connection primarily in the fact that both the play and the masque are concerned with marriage. This is certainly true, but it would be a strange masque performed on the occasion of a nuptial that did *not* concern itself with marriage.
6. Norman A. Brittin, *Thomas Middleton* (New York: Twayne, 1972), p. 128.
7. Inga-Stina Ewbank, "Realism and Morality in 'Women Beware Women,'" *E&S,* 22 (1969), p. 67.
8. My summary of the difficulties of dating these plays draws on Bentley, IV, 862-63, 906-07; Mulryne, Introd., *Women Beware Women,* pp. xxxii-xxxviii; and Bawcutt, Introd., *The Changeling,* pp. xxiv-xxv.
9. Frederick Gard Fleay, *A Biographical Chronicle of the English Drama 1559–1642* (London: Reeves and Turner, 1891), II, 97; Irving Ribner, *Jacobean Tragedy: The Quest for Moral Order* (New York: Barnes and Noble, 1962), p. 124n.
10. "The Date of Middleton's *Women Beware Women,*" *PQ,* 22 (1943), 338-42.
11. Mulryne, pp. xxxviii-li. There is an account of the actual events celebrating this marriage in Leo Schrade, "Les Fêtes du Mariage de Francesco dei Medici et de Bianca Cappello," in *Les Fêtes de la Renaissance,* ed. Jean Jacquot (Paris: Centre National de la Recherche Sci-

entifique, 1956), pp. 107-31. Several etchings from a 1579 account of the wedding are reproduced in Hugh Edwards, "The Marriage of Francesco de' Medici and Bianca Cappello," *Art Institute of Chicago Quarterly*, 46 (1952), pp. 62-67.

12. Mulryne, p. li.
13. Ewbank, "Realism and Morality in 'Women Beware Women,'" p. 69.
14. The dates are those given in the *Annals*.
15. See, for example, Schoenbaum, *Middleton's Tragedies*, p. 126; Mehl, *The Elizabethan Dumb Show*, p. 151; and Mehl, "Forms and Functions," pp. 47-49.
16. Fishman, p. 188.
17. Chambers, III, 442-43.
18. Bentley, IV, 881. R.C. Bald's edition of *Heroes* is included in *A Book of Masques*.
19. Welsford, p. 212.
20. Bentley, IV, 908-09.
21. Welsford, p. 214.
22. Thomas Middleton and William Rowley, *The World Tost at Tennis*, ed. A.H. Bullen, in *The Works of Thomas Middleton*, VII (London: Nimmo, 1886), Prologue, 1; Epilogue, 1-3.
23. Bentley, IV, 909.
24. Ewbank, "'These Pretty Devices,'" p. 446n.
25. Francis Beaumont and John Fletcher, *Philaster or Love Lies a-Bleeding*, ed. Andrew Gurr, Revels (London: Methuen, 1969), 5.3.51-59.
26. It is disappointing to find merely a passing reference to the play's "master-servant clowns" Ward and Sordido in Richard Levin's otherwise comprehensive (especially on Middleton) *The Multiple Plot in English Renaissance Drama* (Chicago: Univ. of Chicago Press, 1971), p. 110n. *Women Beware Women* seems to me a good example of what Levin calls a "three-level hierarchy" (the Leantio-Bianca-Duke plot, the Isabella-Hippolito subplot, and the Guardiano-Ward-Isabella clown plot); see Levin, p. 55.
27. "Throws flaming gold upon Isabella, who falls dead" is the stage direction written in a seventeenth-century hand in Yale's copy of the octavo. Mulryne makes a convincing case for admitting this direction to his critical edition (pp. xxx, 161n). See also his "Annotations in Some Copies of *Two New Playes by Thomas Middleton*, 1657," *The Library*, 30 (1975), 217-21.
28. Ewbank, "Realism and Morality in 'Women Beware Women,'" p. 63.
29. Mulryne, p. 144n.
30. Ewbank, "Realism and Morality in 'Women Beware Women,'" p. 63.
31. Bradbrook, p. 46.
32. Mulryne, in *Women Beware Women*, p. 157 (collation).
33. Mulryne, p. xxx.
34. Parker, p. 198.
35. Ewbank, "Realism and Morality in 'Women Beware Women,'" pp. 68-69.

Chapter 8—Middleton and Rowley's *The Changeling*

1. *Some Versions of Pastoral* (London: Chatto and Windus, 1935), p. 51. Cf. Laird, pp. 136-38; Cornelia, p. 141; George Walton Williams, Introd., *The Changeling*, Regents (Lincoln: Univ. of Nebraska Press, 1966), p. xxiii; and Levin, p. 46n.
2. *Shakespeare and His Fellow Dramatists* (New York: Prentice-Hall, 1929), II, 903.
3. Bawcutt, Introd., *The Changeling*, pp. xvi-xvii.
4. *Thomas Middleton and the Drama of Realism: A Study of Some Representative Plays* (Edinburgh: Oliver and Boyd, 1973), p. 134.
5. Levin, pp. 47-48.
6. Levin, p. 47.
7. This seems to be what Oliphant is suggesting (II, 903).
8. Bawcutt, pp. xxiv-xxviii.
9. Levin, p. 8.
10. Levin, p. 35. Levin's labels, taken from Aristotle's four causes, are defined in his first chapter, pp. 5-20.
11. Empson, p. 50.
12. Bradbrook, p. 221.
13. "The Dramatic Structure of *The Changeling*," in *Renaissance Papers*, ed. Allan H. Gilbert (Columbia: Univ. of South Carolina Press, 1954), pp. 77-87; rpt. in *Shakespeare's Contemporaries: Modern Studies in English Renaissance Drama*, ed. Max Bluestone and Norman Rabkin, 2nd ed. (Englewood Cliffs: Prentice-Hall, 1970), p. 374.
14. Cf. his earlier question to Lollio: "Will all be perfect, think'st thou?" (4.3.53). The word "perfect" had a technical meaning in the Renaissance: the Elizabethan measure was often classified as "perfect," in varying degrees, or "imperfect." See Dolmetsch, p. 7: "The perfection or imperfection depends upon whether the double paces are followed by a second pair of single paces, in which case the measure is *perfect*, or are immediately followed by the reprises and branle, this sequence rendering the measure *imperfect*. The various degrees of perfection, i.e. *very perfect*, *perfect*, and *more than perfect*, depend upon the number of consecutive double paces and reprises grouped in one measure." If, as I think likely, Alibius sees a wild distracted measure and some sort of mad morris, the technical connotation in his announcement that "'Tis perfect" works ironically.
15. Empson, p. 51.
16. Levin, p. 17.
17. If Levin is really seeking Isabella's motive here, there is a perfectly good one in the fact that they are wanted for murder.
18. Bradbrook, p. 221.
19. Farr, p. 134.
20. Cornelia, pp. 143-44.

Epilogue: Woe and Wonder

1. Laird, pp. 140-141.
2. Ewbank, " 'These Pretty Devices,' " p. 448.
3. Orgel, "Antimasque," p. 320.
4. See *Paradoxica Epidemica: The Renaissance Tradition of Paradox* (Princeton: Princeton Univ. Press, 1966).
5. "The Metaphysical Poets" (1921), rpt. in *Selected Essays*, new ed. (New York: Harcourt, Brace, 1950), p. 247.
6. This term is problematic because there is little consensus on how—or even whether—the concept applies to literature. Cyrus Hoy, whose comments on the mannerist tension between the Jacobean court audience and the Jonsonian masque I have quoted, argues that the Jacobean tragedies of Shakespeare, Tourneur, Webster, and Middleton are in the mannerist style. For an overview of current theories and problems of literary and theatrical mannerism, see James V. Mirollo, "The Mannered and the Mannerist in Late Renaissance Literature," in *The Meaning of Mannerism*, ed. Franklin W. Robinson and Stephen G. Nichols, Jr. (Hanover: Univ. Press of New England, 1972), pp. 7-24.
7. *Religio Medici*, II, 4, in *The Prose of Sir Thomas Browne*, ed. Norman Endicott (New York: New York Univ. Press, 1968), p. 73.

Selected Bibliography

Primary Sources

Bacon, Francis. *Francis Bacon: A Selection of His Works*. Ed. Sidney Warhaft. New York: Odyssey, 1965.

Beaumont, Francis, and John Fletcher. *The Maid's Tragedy*. Ed. Andrew Gurr. Fountainwell Drama Texts. Berkeley: Univ. of California Press, 1969.

Beaumont, Francis, and John Fletcher. *The Maid's Tragedy*. Ed. Howard B. Norland. Regents Renaissance Drama Series. Lincoln: Univ. of Nebraska Press, 1968.

Beaumont, Francis, and John Fletcher. *The Maid's Tragedy*. Ed. Robert K. Turner, Jr. In *The Dramatic Works in the Beaumont and Fletcher Canon*. Gen. ed. Fredson Bowers. Vol. 2. Cambridge: Cambridge Univ. Press, 1970.

Beaumont, Francis, and John Fletcher. *Philaster or, Love Lies a-Bleeding*. Ed. Andrew Gurr. The Revels Plays. London: Methuen, 1969.

Browne, Sir Thomas. *The Prose of Sir Thomas Browne*. Ed. Norman Endicott. New York: New York Univ. Press, 1968.

Chapman, George. *The Plays and Poems of George Chapman*. Ed. Thomas Marc Parrott. 2 vols. London: Routledge, 1910–14.

The Geneva Bible: A Facsimile of the 1560 Edition. Introd. Lloyd E. Berry. Madison: Univ. of Wisconsin Press, 1969.

Harrier, Richard C., ed. *The Anchor Anthology of Jacobean Drama*. Vol. 2. Garden City: Anchor, 1963.

Jonson, Ben. *Ben Jonson*. Ed. C.H. Herford and Percy and Evelyn Simpson. 11 vols. Oxford: Clarendon, 1925–52.

Jonson, Ben. *Ben Jonson: The Complete Masques.* Ed. Stephen Orgel. New Haven: Yale Univ. Press, 1969.

Kyd, Thomas. *The Spanish Tragedy.* Ed. Philip Edwards. Revels. Cambridge, Mass.: Harvard Univ. Press, 1959.

Kyd, Thomas. *The Spanish Tragedy.* Ed. J.R. Mulryne. New Mermaids. New York: Hill and Wang, 1970.

Marston, John. *Antonio and Mellida.* Ed. G.K. Hunter. Regents. Lincoln: Univ. of Nebraska Press, 1965.

Marston, John. *Antonio's Revenge.* Ed. W. Reavley Gair. Revels. Baltimore: Johns Hopkins Univ. Press, 1978.

Marston, John. *Antonio's Revenge.* Ed. G.K. Hunter. Regents. Lincoln: Univ. of Nebraska Press, 1965.

Marston, John. *The Malcontent.* Ed. Bernard Harris. New Mermaids. London: Benn, 1967.

Marston, John. *The Plays of John Marston.* Ed. A.H. Bullen. 3 vols. London: Bullen, 1887.

Marston, John. *The Plays of John Marston.* Ed. H. Harvey Wood. 3 vols. Edinburgh: Oliver and Boyd, 1934–39.

Marston, John. *The Poems of John Marston.* Ed. Arnold Davenport. Liverpool: Liverpool Univ. Press, 1961.

Middleton, Thomas. *Women Beware Women.* Ed. Charles Barber. Fountainwell. Berkeley: Univ. of California Press, 1969.

Middleton, Thomas. *Women Beware Women.* Ed. J.R. Mulryne. Revels. London: Methuen, 1975.

Middleton, Thomas. *The Works of Thomas Middleton.* Ed. A.H. Bullen. 8 vols. London: Nimmo, 1885–86; rpt. New York: AMS Press, 1965.

Middleton, Thomas, and William Rowley. *The Changeling.* Ed. N.W. Bawcutt. Revels. London: Methuen, 1958.

Middleton, Thomas, and William Rowley. *The Changeling.* Ed. Matthew W. Black. Philadelphia: Univ. of Pennsylvania Press, 1966.

Middleton, Thomas, and William Rowley. *The Changeling.* Ed. George Walton Williams. Regents. Lincoln: Univ. of Nebraska Press, 1966.

Sackville, Thomas, and Thomas Norton. *Gorboduc, or Ferrex and Porrex.* Ed. Irby B. Cauthen, Jr. Regents. Lincoln: Univ. of Nebraska Press, 1970.

Shakespeare, William. *William Shakespeare: The Complete Works.* Gen. ed. Alfred Harbage. Baltimore: Penguin, 1969.

Spencer, T.J.B., et al., eds. *A Book of Masques in Honour of Allardyce Nicoll.* Cambridge: Cambridge Univ. Press, 1967.

Tourneur, Cyril. *The Revenger's Tragedy.* Ed. R.A. Foakes. Revels. London: Methuen, 1966.

Tourneur, Cyril. *The Revenger's Tragedy.* Ed. Brian Gibbons. New Mermaids. London: Benn, 1967.

Tourneur, Cyril. *The Revenger's Tragedy.* Ed. Lawrence J. Ross. Regents. Lincoln: Univ. of Nebraska Press, 1966.

Tourneur, Cyril. *The Works of Cyril Tourneur.* Ed. Allardyce Nicoll. 1930; rpt. New York: Russell and Russell, 1963.

Webster, John. *The Complete Works of John Webster.* Ed. F.L. Lucas. 4 vols. London: Chatto and Windus, 1927.

Webster, John. *The Duchess of Malfi.* Ed. Elizabeth M. Brennan. New Mermaids. New York: Hill and Wang, 1965.

Webster, John. *The Duchess of Malfi.* Ed. John Russell Brown. Revels. Cambridge: Harvard Univ. Press, 1964.

Webster, John. *The Duchess of Malfi.* Ed. F.L. Lucas. Rev. ed. New York: Macmillan, 1959.

Webster, John. *The White Devil.* Ed. John Russell Brown. Revels. Cambridge, Mass.: Harvard Univ. Press, 1960.

Secondary Sources

Abel, Lionel. *Metatheatre: A New View of Dramatic Form.* New York: Hill and Wang, 1963.

Anglo, Sydney. "The Evolution of the Early Tudor Disguising, Pageant, and Mask." *RenD,* NS 1 (1968), 3–44.

Appleton, William W. *Beaumont and Fletcher: A Critical Study.* London: George Allen and Unwin, 1956.

Armstrong, William A. *Elizabethan Private Theatres: Facts and Problems.* London: Society for Theatre Research, 1958.

Axton, Marie. "The Tudor Mask and Elizabethan Court Drama." In *English Drama: Forms and Development. Essays in Honour of Muriel Clara Bradbrook.* Ed. Marie Axton and Raymond Williams. Cambridge: Cambridge Univ. Press, 1977, pp. 24–47.

Ayres, P.J. "Marston's *Antonio's Revenge*: The Morality of the Revenging Hero." *SEL,* 12 (1972), 359–74.

Barker, Richard Hindry. *Thomas Middleton.* New York: Columbia Univ. Press, 1958.

Barroll, J. Leeds, Alexander Leggatt, Richard Hosley, and Alvin Kernan. *The Revels History of Drama in English, 1576–1613.* Vol. 3. London: Methuen, 1975.

Beckerman, Bernard. *Dynamics of Drama: Theory and Method of Analysis.* New York: Knopf, 1970.

Beckerman, Bernard. *Shakespeare at the Globe, 1599–1609.* New York: Macmillan, 1962.

Bentley, Gerald Eades. *The Jacobean and Caroline Stage.* 7 vols. Oxford: Clarendon, 1941–68.

Bergeron, David M. *Twentieth-Century Criticism of English Masques, Pageants, and Entertainments: 1558–1642.* San Antonio: Trinity Univ. Press, 1972.

Berry, Francis. *The Shakespeare Inset: Word and Picture.* London: Routledge and Kegan Paul, 1965.

Berry, Ralph. *The Art of John Webster.* Oxford: Clarendon, 1972.

Berry, Ralph. "Masques and Dumb Shows in Webster's Plays." *ETh* 7 (1979), 124–46.

Bilton, Peter. *Commentary and Control in Shakespeare's Plays.* Norwegian

Studies in English, 19. New York: Humanities Press, 1974.

Bluestone, Max, and Norman Rabkin, eds. *Shakespeare's Contemporaries: Modern Studies in English Renaissance Drama*. 2nd ed. Englewood Cliffs: Prentice-Hall, 1970.

Boas, F.S. "The Play Within the Play." In *A Series of Papers on Shakespeare and the Theatre*. London: Shakespeare Assn., 1927, pp. 134–56.

Boklund, Gunnar. *The Duchess of Malfi: Sources, Themes, Characters*. Cambridge, Mass.: Harvard Univ. Press, 1962.

Bowers, Fredson. *Elizabethan Revenge Tragedy 1587–1642*. Princeton: Princeton Univ. Press, 1940.

Bradbrook, M.C. *The Living Monument: Shakespeare and the Theatre of His Time*. Cambridge: Cambridge Univ. Press, 1976.

Bradbrook, M.C. *Themes and Conventions of Elizabethan Tragedy*. Cambridge: Cambridge Univ. Press, 1935.

Brittin, Norman A. *Thomas Middleton*. Twayne's English Author Series. New York: Twayne, 1972.

Brodwin, Leonora Leet. *Elizabethan Love Tragedy, 1587–1625*. New York: New York Univ. Press, 1971.

Broude, Ronald. "Human and Divine Vengeance in the Tragedy of Revenge." Diss. Columbia, 1967.

Broude, Ronald. "Revenge and Revenge Tragedy in Renaissance England." *RenQ*, 28 (1975), 38–58.

Broude, Ronald. "*Vindicta Filia Temporis*: Three English Forerunners of the Elizabethan Revenge Play." *JEGP*, 72 (1973), 489–502.

Brown, Arthur. "The Play Within a Play: An Elizabethan Dramatic Device." *E&S*, NS 13 (1960), 36–48.

Brown, John Russell. "The Printing of John Webster's Plays." *SB*, 6 (1954), 117–40; 8 (1956), 113–27; 15 (1962), 57–69.

Brown, John Russell, and Bernard Harris, eds. *Jacobean Theatre*. Stratford-upon-Avon Studies I. London, 1960; rpt. New York: Capricorn, 1967.

Calderwood, James L. *Shakespearean Metadrama: The Argument of the Play in* Titus Andronicus, Love's Labor's Lost, Romeo and Juliet, A Midsummer Night's Dream, *and* Richard II. Minneapolis: Univ. of Minnesota Press, 1971.

Campbell, Lily B. *Scenes and Machines on the English Stage During the Renaissance*. Cambridge, 1923; rpt. New York: Barnes and Noble, 1960.

Chambers, E.K. *The Elizabethan Stage*. 4 vols. Oxford: Clarendon, 1923.

Champion, Larry S. "Tourneur's *The Revenger's Tragedy* and the Jacobean Tragic Perspective." *SP*, 72 (1975), 299–321.

Colie, Rosalie L. *Paradoxica Epidemica: The Renaissance Tradition of Paradox*. Princeton: Princeton Univ. Press, 1966.

Cope, Jackson I. *The Theater and the Dream: From Metaphor to Form in Renaissance Drama*. Baltimore: Johns Hopkins Univ. Press, 1973.

Cornelia, M. Bonaventure, S.S.J. "The Function of the Masque in Jacobean Tragedy and Tragicomedy." Diss. Fordham 1968.

Coursen, Herbert R., Jr. "The Rarer Action: Hamlet's Mousetrap." *Literary Monographs*, 2 (1969), 59–97.

Coursen, Herbert R., Jr. "A Spacious Mirror: Shakespeare and the Play Within." Diss. Connecticut 1965.

Coursen, Herbert R., Jr. "The Unity of *The Spanish Tragedy*." *SP*, 65 (1968), 768–82.

Cox, John D. "*Henry VIII* and the Masque." *ELH*, 45 (1978), 390–409.

Crow, John. "Deadly Sins of Criticism, or, Seven Ways to Get Shakespeare Wrong." *SQ*, 9 (1958), 301–06.

Cunliffe, John W. "Italian Prototypes of the Masque and Dumb Show." *PMLA*, 22 (1907), 140–56.

Cunliffe, John W. "The Masque in Shakespeare's Plays." *Archiv*, 125 (1910), 71–82.

Cunningham, Dolora. "The Jonsonian Masque as a Literary Form." *ELH*, 22 (1955), 108–24. Rpt. in *Ben Jonson: A Collection of Critical Essays*. Ed. Jonas A. Barish. Englewood Cliffs: Prentice-Hall, 1963, pp. 160–74.

Cunningham, J.V. *Woe or Wonder: The Emotional Effect of Shakespearean Tragedy*. Denver: Univ. of Denver Press, 1951.

Cutts, John P. "Jacobean Masque and Stage Music." *M&L*, 35 (1954), 185–200.

Cutts, John P. *La Musique de Scène de la Troupe de Shakespeare: The King's Men Sous le Règne de Jacques Ier*. Paris: Centre National de la Recherche Scientifique, 1959.

Danby, John F. *Poets on Fortune's Hill*. London: Faber and Faber, 1952.

Demaray, John G. *Milton and the Masque Tradition: The Early Poems, "Arcades," and* Comus. Cambridge, Mass.: Harvard Univ. Press, 1968.

Dent, Robert W. *John Webster's Borrowing*. Berkeley: Univ. of California Press, 1960.

De Tervarent, Guy. "*Veritas* and *Justitia* Triumphant." *JWCI*, 7 (1944), 95–101.

Diekhoff, John S., ed. *A Maske at Ludlow: Essays on Milton's "Comus."* Cleveland: Case Western Reserve Univ. Press, 1968.

Dolmetsch, Mabel. *Dances of England and France 1450–1600*. London: Routledge and Paul, 1949.

Dolmetsch, Mabel. *Dances of Spain and Italy from 1400 to 1600*. London: Routledge and Kegan Paul, 1954.

Doran, Madeleine. *Endeavors of Art: A Study of Form in Elizabethan Drama*. Madison: Univ. of Wisconsin Press, 1954.

Edwards, Hugh. "The Marriage of Francesco de' Medici and Bianca Cappello." *The Art Institute of Chicago Quarterly*, 46 (1952), 62–67.

Egan, Robert. *Drama Within Drama: Shakespeare's Sense of His Art in "King Lear," "The Winter's Tale," and "The Tempest."* New York: Columbia Univ. Press, 1975.

Eliot, T.S. *Essays on Elizabethan Drama*. 1932; rpt. New York: Harcourt, Brace, and World, 1960.

Eliot, T.S. *Selected Essays*. New ed. New York: Harcourt, Brace, 1950.

Empson, William. *Some Versions of Pastoral*. London: Chatto and Windus, 1935.

[Ewbank,] Inga-Stina Ekeblad. "An Approach to Tourneur's Imagery." *MLR*, 54 (1959), 489–98.

[Ewbank,] Inga-Stina Ekeblad. "The 'Impure Art' of John Webster." *RES*, NS 9 (1958), 253–67. Rpt. in *John Webster: A Critical Anthology*. Ed. G.K. Hunter and S.K. Hunter. Baltimore: Penguin, 1969, pp. 202–21.

[Ewbank,] Inga-Stina Ekeblad. "On the Authorship of *The Revenger's Tragedy*." *ES*, 41 (1960), 225–40.

Ewbank, Inga-Stina. " 'The Eloquence of Masques': A Retrospective View of Masque Criticism." *RenD*, NS 1 (1968), 307–27.

Ewbank, Inga-Stina. " 'More Pregnantly Than Words': Some Uses and Limitations of Visual Symbols." *ShS*, 24 (1971), 13–18.

Ewbank, Inga-Stina. "Realism and Morality in 'Women Beware Women.' " *E&S*, 22 (1969), 57–70.

Ewbank, Inga-Stina. " 'These Pretty Devices': A Study of Masques in Plays." In *A Book of Masques in Honour of Allardyce Nicoll*. Ed. T.J.B. Spencer, et al. Cambridge: Cambridge Univ. Press, 1967, pp. 405–48.

Faber, D.M., and Colin Skinner. "*The Spanish Tragedy*: Act IV." *PQ*, 49 (1970), 444–59.

Farr, Dorothy M. *Thomas Middleton and the Drama of Realism: A Study of Some Representative Plays*. Edinburgh: Oliver and Boyd, 1973.

Fiedler, Leslie A. "The Defense of the Illusion and the Creation of Myth." In *English Institute Essays 1948*. Ed. D.A. Robertson, Jr. New York: Columbia Univ. Press, 1949, pp. 74–94.

Fieler, Frank B. "The Eight Madmen in *The Duchess of Malfi*." *SEL*, 7 (1967), 343–50.

Finkelpearl, Philip J. *John Marston of the Middle Temple: An Elizabethan Dramatist in His Social Setting*. Cambridge, Mass.: Harvard Univ. Press, 1969.

Fishman, Burton J. "The Fatal Masque: A Study of Visual Metaphor and Dramatic Convention in Renaissance Tragedy." Diss. Princeton 1969.

Fleay, Frederick Gard. *A Biographical Chronicle of the English Drama, 1559–1642*. 2 vols. London, 1891; rpt. New York: Franklin, 1962.

Foakes, R.A. "The Art of Cruelty: Hamlet and Vindice." *ShS*, 26 (1973), 21–31.

Foakes, R.A. "John Marston's Fantastical Plays: *Antonio and Mellida* and *Antonio's Revenge*." *PQ*, 41 (1962), 229–39.

Forsythe, Robert Stanley. *The Relations of Shirley's Plays to the Elizabethan Drama*. New York: Columbia Univ. Press, 1914.

Fuller, David. "The Jonsonian Masque and its Music." *M&L*, 54 (1973), 440–52.

Fuzier, Jean. "La Tragédie de Vengeance Elisabethaine et le Théâtre dans le Théâtre." *RSH*, 145 (1972), 17–33.

Gaw, Allison, "The Impromptu Mask in Shakespeare." *Shakespeare Assn. Bull.*, 11 (1936), 149–60.

Gayley, Charles M. *Beaumont the Dramatist.* New York: Century, 1914.

Gilbert, A. H. "The Function of the Masques in *Cynthia's Revels.*" *PQ,* 22 (1943), 211–30.

Golding, M.R. "Variations in the Use of the Masque in English Revenge Tragedy." *YES,* 3 (1973), 44–54.

Gordon, D.J. "*Hymenaei:* Ben Jonson's Masque of Union." *JWCI,* 8 (1945), 107–45.

Gordon, D.J. "Poet and Architect: The Intellectual Setting of the Quarrel Between Ben Jonson and Inigo Jones." *JWCI,* 12 (1949), 152–78.

Gossett, Suzanne S. "The Influence of the Jacobean Masque on the Plays of Beaumont and Fletcher." Diss. Princeton 1968.

Gossett, Suzanne S. "Masque Influence on the Dramaturgy of Beaumont and Fletcher." *MP,* 69 (1971–72), 199–208.

Gossett, Suzanne S. "The Term 'Masque' in Shakespeare and Fletcher, and *The Coxcomb.*" *SEL,* 14 (1974), 285–95.

Greg, W.W. "The Rationale of Copy-Text." *SB,* 3 (1950–51), 19–36.

Grivelet, Michel. "Shakespeare et 'The Play Within the Play.' " *RSH,* 145 (1972), 35–52.

Gurr, Andrew. *The Shakespearean Stage 1574–1642.* Cambridge: Cambridge Univ. Press, 1970.

Hamilton, Donna B. "*The Spanish Tragedy*: A Speaking Picture." *ELR,* 4 (1974), 203–17.

Harbage, Alfred. *Annals of English Drama 975–1700.* Rev. by S. Schoenbaum. London: Methuen, 1964.

Harbage, Alfred. *Shakespeare and the Rival Traditions.* New York: Macmillan, 1952.

Hauser, Arnold. *Mannerism: The Crisis of the Renaissance and the Origin of Modern Art.* 2 vols. London: Routledge and Kegan Paul, 1965.

Hawkins, Harriet. "Fabulous Counterfeits: Dramatic Construction and Dramatic Perspectives in *The Spanish Tragedy, A Midsummer Night's Dream,* and *The Tempest.*" *ShakS,* 6 (1970), 51–65.

Hawkins, Harriet. *Likenesses of Truth in Elizabethan and Restoration Drama.* Oxford: Clarendon, 1972.

Hayakawa, S. Ichiyé. "A Note on the Madmen's Scene in Webster's *The Duchess of Malfi,*" *PMLA,* 47 (1932), 907–09.

Haydn, Hiram. *The Counter-Renaissance.* New York: Scribner, 1950.

Hedrick, Donald K. "The Masquing Principle in Marston's *The Malcontent.*" *ELR,* 8 (1978), 24–42.

Henkel, Arthur, and Albrecht Schöne. *Emblemata: Handbuch zur Sinnbildkunst des XVI, und XVII, Jahrhunderts.* Stuttgart: Metzler, 1967.

Hermerén, Göran. *Influence in Art and Literature.* Princeton: Princeton Univ. Press, 1975.

Holmes, David M. *The Art of Thomas Middleton: A Critical Study.* Oxford: Clarendon, 1970.

Homan, Sidney. "When the Theater Turns to Itself." *NLH,* 2 (1971), 407–17.

Honigmann, E.A.J. *Shakespeare: Seven Tragedies. The Dramatist's Manipulation of Response.* London: Macmillan, 1976.

Hoy, Cyrus. "Jacobean Tragedy and the Mannerist Style." *ShS,* 26 (1973), 49–67.

Hoy, Cyrus. "Masques and the Artiface of Tragedy." *ETh* 7 (1979), 111–23.

Hoy, Cyrus. "The Shares of Fletcher and His Collaborators in the Beaumont and Fletcher Canon." *SB,* 8 (1956), 129–46; 9 (1957), 143–62; 11 (1958), 85–106; 12 (1959), 91–116; 13 (1960), 77–108; 14 (1961), 45–67; 15 (1962), 71–90.

Huizinga, Johan. *Homo Ludens: A Study of the Play Element in Culture.* Haarlem, 1938; New York: Harper and Row, 1970.

Hunter, G.K. "*Henry IV* and the Elizabethan Two-Part Play." *RES,* 19 (1954), 236–48.

Hunter, G.K., and S.K. Hunter. *John Webster: A Critical Anthology.* Baltimore: Penguin, 1969.

Iser, Wolfgang. "Das Spiel im Spiel. Formen dramatischen Illusion bei Shakespeare." *Archiv,* 198 (1961–62), 209–26.

Jacobs, Henry E. "Theaters Within Theaters: Levels of Dramatic Illusion in Ben Jonson's Comedies." Diss. Indiana Univ. 1974.

Jacquot, Jean. "The Last Plays and the Masque." In *Shakespeare 1971: Proceedings of the World Shakespeare Congress, Vancouver, August 1971.* Ed. Clifford Leech and J. M. R. Margeson. Toronto: Univ. of Toronto Press, 1972, pp. 156–73.

Jacquot, Jean. "Sur la Forme du Masque Jacobéen." *Baroque: Revue Internationale,* 5 (1972), 35–47.

Johnson, S.F. "*The Spanish Tragedy,* or Babylon Revisited." In *Essays on Shakespeare and Elizabethan Drama in Honor of Hardin Craig.* Ed. Richard Hosley. Columbia: Univ. of Missouri Press, 1962, pp. 23–36.

Kirsch, Arthur C. *Jacobean Dramatic Perspectives.* Charlottesville: Univ. Press of Virginia, 1972.

Kirsch, Arthur C. "Jacobean Theatrical Self-Consciousness." *RORD,* 23 (1979), 9–13.

Laird, David. "Hieronimo's Dilemma." *SP,* 62 (1965), 136–46.

Laird, David. "The Inserted Masque in Elizabethan and Jacobean Drama." Diss. Wisconsin 1955.

Lawrence, Robert C. "A Bibliographical Study of Middleton and Rowley's *The Changeling.*" *The Library,* 5th ser., 16 (1961), 37–43.

Lawrence, William John. "Plays Within Plays." *New Shakespeareana,* 3 (1904), 121–27.

Leech, Clifford. *The John Fletcher Plays.* Cambridge: Harvard Univ. Press, 1962.

Lehrman, Walter D. "Courtly Ritual: A Study of the English Masque." Diss. Case Western Reserve Univ. 1972.

Lever, J.W. *The Tragedy of State.* London: Methuen, 1971.

Levin, Richard. *The Multiple Plot in English Renaissance Drama*. Chicago: Univ. of Chicago Press, 1971.

Levin, Richard. *New Readings vs. Old Plays: Recent Trends in the Reinterpretation of English Renaissance Drama*. Chicago: Univ. of Chicago Press, 1979.

Lisca, P. "*The Revenger's Tragedy*: A Study in Irony." *PQ*, 38 (1959), 242–51.

Maxwell, Baldwin. "The Date of Middleton's *Women Beware Women*." *PQ*, 22 (1943), 338–42.

McAlindon, T. *Shakespeare and Decorum*. New York: Harper and Row, 1973.

McCullen, Joseph T., Jr. "Madness and the Isolation of Characters in Elizabethan and Early Stuart Drama." *SP*, 48 (1951), 206–18.

Meagher, John C. "The Dance and the Masques of Ben Jonson." *JWCI*, 25 (1962), 258–77.

Mehl, Dieter. *The Elizabethan Dumb Show: The History of a Dramatic Convention*. Cambridge, Mass.: Harvard Univ. Press, 1966.

Mehl, Dieter. "Emblems in English Renaissance Drama." *RenD*, NS 2 (1969), 39–57.

Mehl, Dieter. "Forms and Functions of the Play Within a Play." *RenD*, 8 (1965), 41–61.

Mehl, Dieter. "Zur Entwicklung des 'Play Within a Play' im elisabethanischen Drama." *SJH*, 97 (1961), 134–52.

Mirollo, James V. "The Mannered and the Mannerist in Late Renaissance Literature." In *The Meaning of Mannerism*. Ed. Franklin W. Robinson and Stephen G. Nichols, Jr. Hanover: Univ. Press of New England, 1972, pp. 7–24.

Mulryne, J.R. "Annotations in Some Copies of *Two New Plays by Thomas Middleton*, 1657." *The Library*, 30 (1975), 217–21.

Murray, Peter B. *A Study of Cyril Tourneur*. Philadelphia: Univ. of Pennsylvania Press, 1964.

Neill, Michael. " 'The Simetry, Which Gives a Poem Grace': Masque, Imagery, and the Fancy of *The Maid's Tragedy*." *RenD*, NS 3 (1970), 111–35.

Nelson, Robert J. *Play Within a Play: The Dramatist's Conception of His Art, Shakespeare to Anouilh*. New Haven: Yale Univ. Press, 1958.

Nicoll, Allardyce. "Shakespeare and the Court Masque." *SJH*, 94 (1958), 51–62.

Nicoll, Allardyce. *Stuart Masques and the Renaissance Stage*. 1938; rpt. New York: Benjamin Blom, 1963.

Norland, Howard N. "The Text of *The Maid's Tragedy*." *PBSA*, 61 (1967), 173–200.

Oliphant, E.H.C. *The Plays of Beaumont and Fletcher*. New Haven: Yale Univ. Press, 1927.

Oliphant, E.H.C. *Shakespeare and His Fellow Dramatists*. 2 vols. New York: Prentice-Hall, 1929.

O'Neill, David G. "The Influence of Music in the Works of John Marston." *M&L*, 53 (1972), 122–33; 293–308; 400–10.

Orgel, Stephen. "Antimasque." *EIC*, 18 (1968), 310–21.

Orgel, Stephen. *The Illusion of Power: Political Theater in the English Renaissance*. Berkeley: Univ. of California Press, 1975.

Orgel, Stephen. *The Jonsonian Masque*. Cambridge, Mass.: Harvard Univ. Press, 1965.

Orgel, Stephen. "The Poetics of Spectacle." *NLH*, 2 (1971), 367–89.

Orgel, Stephen, and Roy C. Strong. *Inigo Jones: The Theatre of the Stuart Court*. 2 vols. London: Sotheby-Parke Bernet, 1973.

Ornstein, Robert. *The Moral Vision of Jacobean Tragedy*. Madison: Univ. of Wisconsin Press, 1960.

Panofsky, Erwin. *Studies in Iconology: Humanistic Themes in the Art of the Renaissance*. Rev. ed. 1962; rpt. New York: Harper and Row, 1972.

Peter, John. "John Marston's Plays." *Scrutiny*, 17 (1950), 132–53.

Peter, John. "*The Revenger's Tragedy* Reconsidered." *EIC*, 6 (1956), 131–43.

Rabkin, Norman, ed. *Twentieth Century Interpretations of "The Duchess of Malfi:" A Collection of Critical Essays*. Englewood Cliffs: Prentice-Hall, 1968.

Reed, Robert Rentoul, Jr. *Bedlam on the Jacobean Stage*. Cambridge, Mass.: Harvard Univ. Press, 1952.

Reyher, Paul. *Les Masques anglais: Etude sur les ballets et la vie de cour en Angleterre, 1512–1640*. Paris, 1909; rpt. New York: Benjamin Blom, 1964.

Ribner, Irving. *Jacobean Tragedy: The Quest for Moral Order*. New York: Barnes and Noble, 1962.

Righter, Anne. *Shakespeare and the Idea of the Play*. London, 1962; rpt. Baltimore: Penguin, 1967.

Sabol, Andrew J., ed. *Four Hundred Songs and Dances from the Stuart Masque*. Providence: Brown Univ. Press, 1978.

Sabol, Andrew J., ed. *Songs and Dances for the Stuart Masque: An Edition of Sixty-three Items of Music for the English Court Masque from 1604 to 1641*. Providence: Brown Univ. Press, 1959.

Salingar, L.G. " 'The Revenger's Tragedy' and the Morality Tradition." *Scrutiny*, 6 (1938), 402–24.

Sanders, Leslie. "*The Revenger's Tragedy*: A Play on the Revenge Play." *Ren&R*, 10 (1974), 25–36.

Saxl, Fritz. "*Veritas Filia Temporis*." In *Philosophy and History: Essays Presented to Ernst Cassirer*. Ed. Raymond Klibansky and H. J. Paton. Oxford: Clarendon, 1936, pp. 197–222.

Schoenbaum, Samuel. *Middleton's Tragedies: A Critical Study*. New York: Columbia Univ. Press, 1955.

Schoenbaum, Samuel. "Peut-on parler d'une 'décadence' du théâtre au temps des premiers Stuarts?" In *Dramaturgie et Société*. Ed. Jean

Jacquot. Vol. 2. Paris: Centre National de la Recherche Scientifique, 1968, pp. 829−45.

Schoenbaum, Samuel. "*The Revenger's Tragedy*: Jacobean Dance of Death." *MLQ*, 15 (1954), 201−07.

Schrade, Leo. "Les Fêtes du Mariage de Francesco dei Medici et de Bianca Cappello." In *Les Fêtes de la Renaissance*. Ed. Jean Jacquot. Paris: Centre National de la Recherche Scientifique, 1956, pp. 107−31.

Schuman, Samuel. " 'Theatre of Fine Devices': The Visual Imagery of Webster's Tragedy." *Ren&R* 4 (1979), 87−94.

Schwab, Hans. *Das Schauspiel im Schauspiel zur Zeit Shaksperes*. Weiner Beiträge zur englischen Philologie, Band 5. Wein-Leipzig: Braumüller, 1896.

Shapiro, Michael. *Children of the Revels: The Boy Companies of Shakespeare's Time and Their Plays*. New York: Columbia Univ. Press, 1977.

Shaw, Catherine M. "The Dramatic Function of the Masque in English Drama, 1592−1642." Diss. Texas 1967.

Shearman, John. *Mannerism*. Baltimore: Penguin, 1967.

Simmons, J.L. "The Tongue and Its Office in *The Revenger's Tragedy*." *PMLA*, 92 (1977), 56−68.

Smith, Irwin. "Ariel and the Masque in *The Tempest*." *SQ*, 21 (1970), 213−22.

Soergel, Alfred. "Die englischen Maskenspiel." Diss. Halle 1882.

Stilling, Roger. *Love and Death in Renaissance Tragedy*. Baton Rouge: Louisiana State Univ. Press, 1976.

Strong, Roy. *Splendor at Court: Renaissance Spectacle and the Theater of Power*. Boston: Houghton Mifflin, 1973.

Sullivan, Mary. *Court Masques of James I: Their Influence on Shakespeare and the Public Theatres*. New York: Putnam, 1913.

Thorndike, A. H. "The Influence of the Court Masque on the Drama, 1608−1615." *PMLA*, 15 (1900), 114−20.

Tilley, Morris Palmer. *A Dictionary of the Proverbs in England in the Sixteenth and Seventeenth Centuries*. Ann Arbor: Univ. of Michigan Press, 1950.

Tomlinson, T.B. "The Morality of Revenge: Tourneur's Critics." *EIC*, 10 (1960), 134−37.

Turner, Robert K., Jr. "The Printing of Beaumont and Fletcher's *The Maid's Tragedy* Q1 (1619)." *SB*, 13 (1960), 199−220.

Turner, Robert K., Jr. "The Relationship of *The Maid's Tragedy* Q1 and Q2." *PBSA*, 51 (1957), 322−27.

Turner, Robert K., Jr. "A Textual Study of Beaumont and Fletcher's *The Maid's Tragedy*." 2 vols. Diss. Univ. of Virginia 1958.

Tuve, Rosemond. *Images and Themes in Five Poems by Milton*. Cambridge, Mass.: Harvard Univ. Press, 1957.

Van Laan, Thomas F. *Role-Playing in Shakespeare*. Toronto: Univ. of Toronto Press, 1978.

Venezky, Alice S. *Pageantry on the Shakespearean Stage*. New York: Twayne, 1951.

Voight, Joachim. "Das Spiel im Spiel: Versuch einer Formbestimmung an Beispielen aus dem deutschen, englischen, und spanischen Drama." Diss. Göttingen 1954.

Waith, Eugene M. *The Herculean Hero in Marlowe, Chapman, Shakespeare and Dryden*. New York: Columbia Univ. Press, 1962.

Walton, Charles Edward. "The Impact of the Court Masque and the Blackfriars Theatre upon the Staging of Elizabethan-Jacobean Drama." Diss. Missouri 1952.

Warnke, Frank J. *Versions of Baroque: European Literature in the Seventeenth Century*. New Haven: Yale Univ. Press, 1972.

Welsford, Enid. *The Court Masque: A Study in the Relationship Between Poetry and the Revels*. Cambridge, 1927; rpt. New York: Russell and Russell, 1962.

Wickham, Glynne. "Masque and Anti-Masque in *The Tempest*." *E&S*, 28 (1975), 1−14.

Wickham, Glynne. *Shakespeare's Dramatic Heritage: Collected Studies in Mediaeval, Tudor and Shakespearean Drama*. New York: Barnes and Noble, 1969.

Wierum, Ann. " 'Actors' and 'Play Acting' in the Morality Tradition." *RenD*, NS 3 (1970), 189−214.

Wilds, Lillian. *Shakespeare's Character-Dramatists: A Study of a Character Type in Shakespearean Tragedy through Hamlet*. Salzburg Studies in English Literature: Elizabethan and Renaissance Studies, 46. Salzburg: Institut für englische Sprache und Literatur, 1975.

Willson, Robert F., Jr. "The Plays Within *A Midsummer Night's Dream* and *The Tempest*." *SJW*, 110 (1974), 101−11.

Wright, Louis B. "Madmen as Vaudeville Performers on the Elizabethan Stage." *JEGP*, 30 (1931), 48−54.

Index